ADVANCE ACCLAIM FOR *THE PROMISE*

"The story of Mallory in *The Promise* uncovers the harsh reality American women can experience when they follow their hearts into a very different culture. Her story sheds light on how Islamic society is totally different from the Christian marriage covenant between one man and one woman. This novel is based on actual events, and Beth reached out to me during that time. It was heartbreaking to watch those real-life events unfolding. I salute the author's courage, persistence, and final triumph in writing a revealing and inspiring story."

—NONIE DARWISH, AUTHOR OF *THE DEVIL WE DON'T KNOW*, *CRUEL AND USUAL PUNISHMENT*, AND *NOW THEY CALL ME INFIDEL*

"The Promise is an only too realistic depiction of an American young woman motivated by the best humanitarian impulses and naïve trust facing instead betrayal, kidnapping, and life-threatening danger in Pakistan's lawless Pashtun tribal regions. But the story offers as well a reminder just as realistic that love and sacrifice are never wasted and that the hope of a loving heavenly Father is never absent in the most hopeless of situations."

—JEANETTE WINDLE, AUTHOR OF *VEILED FREEDOM* (2010 ECPA CHRISTIAN BOOK AWARD/CHRISTY AWARD FINALIST), *FREEDOM'S STAND* (2012 ECPA CHRISTIAN BOOK AWARD/CAROL AWARD FINALIST), AND *CONGO DAWN* (2013 GOLDEN SCROLL NOVEL OF THE YEAR)

ACCLAIM FOR BETH WISEMAN

THE HOUSE THAT LOVE BUILT

"This sweet story with a hint of mystery is touching and emotional. Humor sprinkled throughout balances the occasional seriousness. The development of the love story is paced perfectly so that the reader gets a real sense of the characters."

—*ROMANTIC TIMES*, 4-STAR REVIEW

"[The House That Love Built] is a warm, sweet tale of faith renewed and families restored."

—BOOKPAGE

"Wiseman, best known for her series of Amish novels, branches out into a wider world in this story of family, dependence, faith, and small-town Texas, offering a character for every reader to relate to . . . With an enjoyable cast of outside characters, *Need You Now* breaks the molds of small-town stereotypes. With issues ranging from special education and teen cutting to what makes a marriage strong, this is a compelling and worthy read."

—Booklist

"Wiseman gets to the heart of marriage and family interests in a way that will resonate with readers, with an intricately written plot featuring elements that seem to be ripped from current headlines. God provides hope for Wiseman's characters even in the most desperate situations."

—Romantic Times, 4-star review

"Wiseman gets to the heart of marriage and family issues in a way that will resonate with readers . . ."

—Romantic Times

"With issues ranging from special education and teen cutting to what makes a marriage strong, this is a compelling and worthy read."

—Booklist

"You may think you are familiar with Beth's wonderful story-telling gift but this is something new! This is a story that will stay with you for a long, long time. It's a story of hope when life seems hopeless. It's a story of how God can redeem the seemingly unredeemable. It's a message the Church, the world needs to hear."

—Sheila Walsh, author of *God Loves Broken People*

"Beth Wiseman tackles these difficult subjects with courage and grace. She reminds us that true healing can only come by being vulnerable and honest before our God who loves us more than anything."

—Deborah Bedford, bestselling author of *His Other Wife*, *A Rose by the Door*, and *The Penny* (coauthored with Joyce Meyer)

The Land of Canaan Novels

"Wiseman's voice is consistently compassionate and her words flow smoothly."

—PUBLISHERS WEEKLY REVIEW OF SEEK ME
WITH ALL YOUR HEART

"Wiseman's third Land of Canaan novel overflows with romance, broken promises, a modern knight in shining armor and hope at the end of the rainbow."

—ROMANTIC TIMES

"In *Seek Me with All Your Heart*, Beth Wiseman offers readers a heart-warming story filled with complex characters and deep emotion. I instantly loved Emily, and eagerly turned each page, anxious to learn more about her past—and what future the Lord had in store for her."

—SHELLEY SHEPARD GRAY, BESTSELLING
AUTHOR OF THE SEASONS OF SUGARCREEK
SERIES

"Wiseman has done it again! Beautifully compelling, *Seek Me with All Your Heart* is a heart-warming story of faith, family, and renewal. Her characters and descriptions are captivating, bringing the story to life with the turn of every page."

—AMY CLIPSTON, BESTSELLING AUTHOR
OF *A GIFT OF GRACE*

The Daughters of the Promise Novels

"Well-defined characters and story make for an enjoyable read."

—ROMANTIC TIMES REVIEW OF
PLAIN PURSUIT

"A touching, heartwarming story. Wiseman does a particularly great job of dealing with shunning, a controversial Amish practice that seems cruel and unnecessary to outsiders . . . If you're a fan of Amish fiction, don't miss *Plain Pursuit*!"

—KATHLEEN FULLER, AUTHOR OF
THE MIDDLEFIELD FAMILY NOVELS

THE
PROMISE

ALSO BY BETH WISEMAN

THE
PROMISE

B ETH W ISEMAN

T HOMAS N ELSON
Since 1798

NASHVILLE   MEXICO CITY   RIO DE JANEIRO

Published in Nashville, Tennessee. Thomas Nelson is a registerd trademark of HarperCollins Christian Publishing, Inc..

Thomas Nelson, Inc., titles may be purchased in bulk for educational, business, fund-raising, or sales promotional use. For information, please e-mail SpecialMarkets@ThomasNelson.com.

Cover Design: Olga Grlic
Cover Photography: Micah Kandros

Publisher's Note: This novel is a work of fiction. Names, characters, places, and incidents are either products of the author's imagination or used fictitiously. All characters are fictional, and any similarity to people living or dead is purely coincidental.

Library of Congress Cataloging-in-Publication Data

Wiseman, Beth, 1962-
  The promise / Beth Wiseman.
    pages cm
  ISBN 978-1-4016-8595-9 (paperback)
  1. Pakistan--Fiction. I. Title.
  PS3623.I83P76 2014
  813'.6--dc23

2014011028

Printed in the United States of America

14 15 16 17 18 RRD 6 5 4 3 2 1

To Laurie. A brave —
and gentle — soul.

PROLOGUE

Mallory slipped into her cousin's hospital room and tiptoed to the side of her bed. Today, about to burst with good news, she barely noticed the antiseptic smell. She sat down in the chair by the bed and scooted close.

"Hey, Kels. You awake?"

Kelsey opened her brown eyes. This was the third time she'd been admitted in the past two months. "Just resting. The doctor says I can go home tomorrow. They're just monitoring me. My blood pressure got too low again after dialysis."

Mallory nodded. They'd been through this before. She handed Kelsey a McDonald's bag. "I checked with the nurse. She said you can have this."

Kelsey smiled. "What would I do without you?"

Even worse . . . what would I do without you?

Mallory and Kelsey had been born three days apart, in this very hospital, and Mallory felt closer to her cousin than to her own sister.

Kelsey held the bag in her lap, but she didn't open it.

"Feeling nauseous?" Mallory asked. "Maybe you'll feel like eating it later."

Kelsey put the bag on the table next to her. "I'm sure I will. You know the food here is awful." She sighed. "I hate this. I know the dialysis is keeping me alive, but I'm so sick of feeling sick."

"You'll be better soon, Kels, I promise."

"You can't promise that. Unless I get a donor—"

"I can't wait another minute!" Mallory reached across the bed and latched onto Kelsey's hand. "I'm not supposed to say anything until I talk to Mom and Dad, but . . ."

Kelsey sat up in the bed, tears filling her eyes. "Are you . . . are you a match?"

Mallory nodded, tears running down her face as well. She had made it through the third round of testing—the only one out of all the friends and family.

"Yes! They just called me on my cell." She threw her arms around her cousin. "I can give you a kidney!"

CHAPTER ONE

Mallory handed Rosa her empty plate. "As usual, dessert was awesome." The food was what kept the mandatory Sunday dinners at her parents' house bearable.

Rosa nodded. Though her dark hair was now speckled with gray, her smile still revealed her girlish dimples and laugh crinkles around her bright eyes. "Glad you liked it, Munchkin."

Mallory smiled at the maid's use of the pet name after all these years.

Rosa went around the table to pick up dessert plates, but Mallory's sister, Vicky, was still working on her key lime pie. Though Mallory missed seeing Haley and Braiden, who were with their father today, she was glad Vicky's children weren't present in case things were about to get ugly.

"Mom, Dad . . . there's something I need to tell you." Mallory's stomach churned and her voice was shaky.

Her mother set down her wineglass. Mallory was pretty sure she'd seen Rosa fill it four times.

"What is it?" Her mother raised her eyebrows. Eyebrows that seemed to be higher up on her forehead. And the tiny lines of time that feathered from each of her eyes had disappeared as well. Mallory was studying the changes, not sure if she liked them or not, when her mother cleared her throat. "What do you need to tell us, Mallory?"

She swallowed hard. "I'm donating one of my kidneys."

Her father sat taller, his eyes sharp and assessing. Vicky halted her fork midway to her mouth, glancing back and forth between their parents. Her mother slammed a palm against the table, shaking the dishes that hadn't yet been cleared.

"No! We're not going through this again." Mom shook her head as she glared at Mallory.

"Mom, I'm an adult. And I've made my decision."

Her mother put her empty wineglass on the table, then pointed a finger at her daughter. "I knew this was why you took a job working for that man. This has never been about utilizing your business degree."

Mallory looked at her father. "Dad, please tell me you understand why I want to do this."

Her father leaned back against his chair and sighed. "Of course I understand, Mallory. But it's a dangerous procedure, and you're our daughter. You need to understand how we feel too."

"I get that, Dad. I really do. But I'm going ahead. I've signed up in a paired kidney exchange program."

Mallory's mother blinked her eyes a few times as she raised

her chin. "This isn't the only way to help. Do you have any idea how much money I have collected over the years through fund-raisers? Money specifically for the Kidney Foundation."

"Mom." Mallory sighed. "That's wonderful. But this isn't a problem that you can just throw money at. People have to make real sacrifices to save lives."

"Did that Muslim put you up to this?" Her mother looked around for Rosa, then pointed at her glass again.

"That is beyond offensive." Mallory glared at her. "I'm going to write that comment off to the wine."

"They *do* all hate us, you know." Vicky eased a piece of pie onto her fork. "We're all infidels to them. They want us all dead."

"You don't even know what you're talking about," Mallory said to her sister. "Ismail is a doctor. He's in the business of saving lives, not taking them."

"That's enough." Dad lifted both his palms, and after he slowly lowered them, he said, "We can't control what you do, honey."

Not this time.

"But we want to make sure you've thought this through." He laid his napkin on his plate.

Mallory blinked back tears. "I've had twelve years to think it through. And I made a promise to Kelsey."

TATE SLID OFF THE PIANO BENCH AND WENT TO THE door. "Why don't you use your key, babe?" he asked, stepping aside so Mallory could come in.

She leaned up and kissed him. "Because I don't live here."

"Then move in." He smiled, knowing what she would say. He'd asked plenty of times.

Mallory sat down on the couch and leaned her head back, giving her blond waves a toss. She closed her eyes. "Your mother would have a fit."

Tate made a quick scan of the room and found ET curled up in the corner behind the rocking chair. Twice the orange-and-white tabby had mistaken Mallory's hair for a plaything when she'd draped it over the back of the couch.

"She'd get over it. You know she loves you." Tate sat down beside her. "So how'd it go?"

Mallory inhaled a big gulp of air, blew it out slowly, and turned to face him. She pulled all her hair over her right shoulder and started braiding it. Tate knew she'd braid it to the end, undo it, and run her fingers through it. Then probably braid it again. It was something she did when she was nervous or upset.

"It went about how I figured it would. Mom went nuts, Vicky made a stupid comment, and Dad tried to keep the peace."

Tate reached for her hand and gave it a squeeze.

"I know you don't want me to do this either. But at least you understand, right?"

Tate kicked his shoeless feet up on the coffee table. "Yeah, I understand. But you blame yourself too much. You were only seventeen. Your parents made the decision."

She was quiet for a while, then sighed. "Maybe I didn't

fight hard enough. Maybe if I'd been more insistent, they would have agreed. And Kelsey would be alive right now."

Tate shook his head. "No. Don't do that to yourself. Your parents made a choice not to let their seventeen-year-old child have major surgery."

"I guess. But I was the youngest one tested. Girls of child-bearing age are never even considered as donors, but since we already knew I couldn't have children, there was no worry about a high-risk pregnancy down the line. I was the perfect person to do it."

Tate waited. He knew about Mallory's condition, of course, and had assured her that it wasn't going to bother him not to have children. If she wanted to adopt someday, fine, but he wasn't sure he was father material anyway. He'd been around kids plenty when he'd taught music at the junior high, and most of his piano students now were children.

"Anyway, no one else was a match. And I had a young, healthy kidney that would have saved Kelsey's life. When I couldn't give that to her, I made a promise that I'd save another life since I couldn't save hers."

"I know. But it wasn't a promise she asked you to make."

Mallory leaned her head on his shoulder, and he wrapped an arm around her and kissed her on the cheek.

"I want to make a difference."

"You do make a difference, each and every day. Just by being you."

She snuggled in closer. "Do you know how much I love you, Tater Tot?"

Tate grinned. "You know how I feel about that name." It seemed unmanly not to put up a little resistance.

She looked up at him with her big, blue eyes and batted her lashes. "I think you secretly love it."

Tate smiled. "Do ya now?"

ET padded across the living room floor, stopping to yawn before he continued on to a small bed in the corner. Tate yawned as well.

"Nap time? I'm guessing you and your mother went to Mass, then to IHOP. You ordered two pancakes and some fruit. And instead of syrup, you put honey on your pancakes." She nodded toward the front window. "Then you came home and mowed the yard." She glanced at her watch. "So, this would make it nap time."

Tate frowned. "Wow. You make me sound so OCD."

She giggled. "No. Just structured."

Tate supposed that in comparison to Mallory, he probably was a little obsessive-compulsive. But it gave him comfort to stay organized and on a schedule. Mallory just winged it and lived spontaneously, on the edge.

"But that's why we complement each other," she added. "That whole opposites attract thing—maybe there's something to it."

"Maybe," he said, half yawning again. He pulled her closer. "You gonna take a nap with me?" As tired as he was, sleep wasn't his top priority.

"I'm not tired," she said with a grin. "But you go ahead."

What he really needed was a distraction. He glanced at his cell phone on the end table. He'd even kept it on vibrate during Mass so he wouldn't miss a call. He wasn't sure if no news was good news. Either way, he'd chosen not to say anything to Mallory yet. If he was offered the job in Chicago, it was really going to shake things up for the two of them.

"Why don't you play something for me? Something pretty and soothing," she said softly.

Tate eased his arm from around her and made his way across the small room to his first love: the baby grand that had been a gift from his uncle nearly thirteen years ago. The black finish shone as brightly today as it did back then. He slid onto the bench and lowered his fingers to the keys and played one of the many songs he'd written for Mallory.

Once again she closed her eyes and leaned her head back against the couch.

Tate stopped abruptly when his cell phone started to ring.

"Aren't you going to get that?" She slid to the end of the couch and peered down at the caller ID. "Chicago Academy for the Arts? Why would they be calling you?"

Tate swallowed hard but didn't move. Was calling him on a Sunday afternoon going to be good news or bad?

CHAPTER TWO

Mallory picked up her pace on the treadmill but didn't bother to dab at the sweat beading on her forehead and dribbling down her cheeks.

"Are you going to tell me what's bothering you?" Soraya had kept a steady pace alongside, though she'd barely broken a sweat. "You should tell me before you pass out." She turned to Mallory and grinned.

Mallory knew that if anyone could cheer her up, it was Soraya, but still she hesitated.

The two women had met at a Pilates class six months earlier. Soraya was from Lahore, where she'd led a privileged life with her family in Pakistan before moving to the United States ten years ago. She was engaged to Ismail, Mallory's boss, and it was she who'd told Mallory about the job opening in his office.

Mallory wasn't sure her friend would understand her dilemma. She lowered the incline on the treadmill and kicked the speed back a few notches. "Tate might have a job offer in Chicago."

"Oh." Soraya's eyes widened a little. "And of course you would move with him."

Mallory hung her head for a moment before she looked back at her friend. "I—I don't know. I—I love Tate. With all my heart. I can't imagine being with anyone else." She sighed.

"There is a *but* in there somewhere," Soraya said as she smiled again.

"I love my job." Mallory raised her shoulders and lowered them slowly as she reached for the towel she had draped over the handrail.

"Of course you do. Who wouldn't love working for my Ismail?" She winked at Mallory.

"You're right to be proud of him, Soraya. He exudes positive energy in everything he does, and he's a great doctor." Mallory caught her breath as she settled into a steady cooldown. "You know that if something happened—and I did have to quit—I would give Ismail plenty of notice."

Soraya raised a sculpted eyebrow. "I know this. I would tell you that there are many Ismails out there to work for"— she pushed her bottom lip into a pout—"but that would be a lie. However . . . you must ask yourself how many Tates are out there. And, by the way, when am I to meet this fabulous fellow?"

"Soon. The four of us need to get together. And I know you're right. I can't imagine my life without Tate."

Soraya finally slowed down on the treadmill, her thick, dark ponytail bouncing in step with her. "I would follow my Ismail to the end of the earth." Her dark eyes lit up when she talked about her fiancé.

"Sounds like you are doing exactly that. I know when the wedding is here, but when is the second celebration?" Mallory knew how much effort was going into the two wedding ceremonies Soraya and Ismail were planning. One here in Houston, the other in their homeland.

"Two months after the one here." Soraya took a sip from her water bottle. Mallory's had been empty for at least the past ten minutes.

Soraya worked out daily, while getting to Pilates once a week was a struggle for Mallory, and the gym was a hit or miss. She thought about Tate and his exercise ritual.

"Right now I am trying to stay focused on our trip to Italy," Soraya added.

They were leaving soon, and Ismail had asked Mallory if she could feed his fish while they were away.

"Ismail seems excited about it."

"Positano is one of my most favorite places in the world, and Ismail has never been there. We considered it for our honeymoon, but we could both use a vacation right now. And Ismail wants to go to Hawaii for our honeymoon."

Soraya stepped off the platform and picked up her phone from the holding area on the treadmill. "No e-mails. No texts. No missed calls." She set it back down and smiled. "Good. I don't want work getting in the way of lunch today. I do believe there is a crème brûlée with my name on it somewhere." She brought a hand to her chest and let out a small gasp. "Can you even imagine life without crème brûlée?"

Mallory knew her friend had fasted for Ramadan, so maybe that explained her appetite today. Although, Mallory wasn't sure she'd ever seen Soraya pass on dessert, and yet she was in great shape. *Note to self—more exercise.*

"It's my favorite dessert too." Mallory sighed as she ran her small towel across her face. "But I might as well slap it to my thighs."

"Life is too short, my friend." Soraya started toward the locker room. Mallory followed. "Which brings me to another point," Soraya said over her shoulder. "Why haven't you and Tate made plans to marry? You've been dating four years."

Mallory was still trying to catch her breath. "Tate wants to get married."

"And you don't?" Soraya raised an eyebrow again as she turned and waited for Mallory to catch up.

Mallory shrugged as Soraya opened the door to the dressing and shower room. "I can't imagine marrying anyone else. Tate is the only man I've ever loved. I mean, I dated guys in high school and college, but I never felt anything like this." She smiled. "Tate is amazing."

"Hmm . . . I'm not sure you answered my question."

"Of course I want to marry him. Just not yet. There are things I want to check off my list first."

"Ismail tells me that you have signed up in the kidney exchange program. He also told me the reason you want to do this. A promise you made to your cousin." Soraya pulled a bag from her locker, then moved toward the shower. "So is this one of the things you are checking off your list?"

"Yes." Mallory looked at the time on her phone and knew she'd need to shower quickly and hurry back to the clinic. She'd sacrificed lunch to work out. "And I don't want anyone telling me I can't do it. I'm not saying that Tate could or would forbid me from doing it, but . . ." She paused. "But he isn't happy about it."

"I understand that. He loves you, so naturally he is worried. He thinks of you as the mother of his future children, yes?"

"That's not in the cards, Soraya. I've known since I was fifteen that I can't have children. Tate knows, of course. It doesn't bother him."

Soraya stared at Mallory. "You've never mentioned that before. I'm sorry, Mallory."

"I've had a long time to get used to the idea."

Soraya shook her head. "We never know what Allah's plan for us is."

Mallory wasn't sure that God had a plan for her. If He did, He needed to go back to the drawing board and make some adjustments.

THE DOORBELL RANG JUST AS TATE WAS SCOOPING ET his usual ration of dog food. Crazy cat wouldn't eat anything else. He glanced at the clock on the wall. Verdell. Tate sent up a quick prayer for patience as he crossed the living room.

"Hello, Verdell." He forced a smile as the boy walked past him, knowing how Verdell would respond.

"Hello, Mr. Webber." Verdell shuffled to the piano, head hung low, as if he were walking a plank. He put his lesson book against the stand and sat down.

Verdell's blond hair was cut high above his ears with a noticeable cowlick that caused a few strands to spike on the top of his head. He was a skinny kid at that awkward age, teeth too big for his mouth. And for reasons Tate didn't understand, Verdell often stole weird things. Little things. Like Tate's toothbrush one week. And a week before that, a bottle of Visine. At first Tate thought he was imagining it, but they were items he would hardly misplace—and Verdell was the only one of his students who always asked to use the bathroom.

"Did you practice this week?" Tate sat down in his chair next to the piano bench. Verdell had a baby grand at his aunt's home too—a Steinway. Tate's dream piano. *For a kid who hates to play.*

"No, I didn't practice, Mr. Webber." Verdell sat taller, his chin in the air and his lips clamped tight.

Tate felt sorry for the child. Both his parents had been killed in a boating accident the previous year, and his aunt was raising him. Tate had told Chantal that she was wasting her money by sending her nephew for lessons, that Verdell had no interest in the piano despite the potential for being good at it. But Chantal begged Tate to keep trying.

Verdell settled his hands on the keys, looked at the music in front of him, then played every note and rhythm perfectly. Like a machine without an ounce of passion for the music.

Tate stood up and paced as he rubbed his forehead. "Do you want to try an exercise in a different book?"

"It doesn't matter." Verdell turned the page and started playing the easy song in front of him. When he was done, he put his hands at his sides. "What now?"

Tate knew he needed to try a different approach. One of the reasons he'd quit his job as a band director was so that he could focus exclusively on piano. He'd dreamily assumed that his private students would all come to their lessons with excitement and a passion for the craft. He sighed as he thought again about the job possibility in Chicago. It would put him back in a classroom setting, but the students were all gifted players who'd fought hard for one of the coveted spots. Mallory hadn't said much when he'd told her about it. Lots to consider for both of them.

"Verdell, I know you hate coming here." Tate decided to just throw it out there and see what happened.

Verdell kept his eyes straight ahead. "Chantal needs time to have her hair done on Mondays. Sometimes her nails. Sometimes a massage." He shrugged. "Or whatever else she likes to do."

Tate had suspected as much. He was being paid to baby-sit for an hour a week.

"Why do you hate the piano so much?"

"I never said that." Verdell twisted sideways on the bench until he was facing Tate.

"So what interests you?"

Verdell glanced toward the window. "Driving your car interests me."

Tate looked out the window at his white Toyota, then grinned when he saw the hint of a smile on the boy's face. "Driving *my* car, or just any car?"

"Any car would be okay."

"Well, you're not old enough to drive. What else?"

Verdell shrugged. "That's about it, I guess."

Verdell turned the page, placed his hands on the keys, and pounded out the next song in the book, each methodical stream of notes like a vise tightening around Tate's head. In a survival method he'd learned early on in his teaching career, Tate allowed himself to check out, this time drifting into a world of what-ifs.

What if I get the job? What if I don't get the job? What if I ask Mallory to marry me and go with me? Will she say yes? What if she says no?

CHAPTER THREE

Ismail checked his roster for the day, then glanced at his watch. He had about thirty minutes before his first patient was scheduled, so he picked up his niece's medical report to study. Abdul had e-mailed it only this morning, but his cousin had already called twice to get Ismail's feedback. Ismail planned to have a hematologist look it over, but at first glance it did appear that Majida's leukemia was at an advanced stage.

His cell phone vibrated on his desk, and he glanced at the ID and sighed.

"Hello, Abdul. I'm just now looking over the report."

His cousin started speaking to him in Urdu. Ismail interrupted him. "Abdul, you're going too fast. I can't understand you."

"News for my Majida is not that of good you will tell me."

Ismail was used to delivering bad news, but it was always more difficult when it was family. And even more so when it was a child.

"I'm going to have a specialist look at Majida's report, a hematologist. But it does look like her condition is quite serious." He rubbed his forehead. The sixteen-year-old was unlikely to get good health care in Peshawar. But money talked in Pakistan, and if Majida was going to have a chance at survival, Abdul was going to need money. And lots of it. Even though Ismail hadn't seen his cousin in fifteen years, he couldn't imagine that Abdul had worked his way into a better financial situation. There just wasn't much opportunity in their homeland, and Ismail lived each day feeling fortunate and blessed that he was no longer there.

"Abdul, I think you should bring Majida to the United States for treatment." Ismail spoke slowly. "Is she well enough to travel? Is this something you or Fozia might be able to do?" He stood up and walked to the window. Opening the blinds, he could see the medical center from his office. "There is a hospital here called MD Anderson. It is the best facility in the world for Majida to receive treatment. Texas Children's Hospital is another possibility. It is also here in Houston. The Children's Hospital usually doesn't turn anyone away."

After a few moments of silence, Ismail said, "Abdul, I can purchase plane tickets for either you or Fozia to bring Majida here."

His cousin started speaking in Urdu again, but Ismail was only getting bits and pieces.

"Abdul, Abdul. You are going too fast again."

His cousin slowed down and spoke to him in chopped English, explaining the reasons he couldn't get travel visas for himself and Majida. Ismail knew that it was hard to get out of Pakistan these days, much harder than when he'd left prior to 9/11.

"Does that apply to Fozia as well?" He wasn't sure if it was any easier for a woman to get a visa to the United States. Sometimes an American could sponsor someone from Pakistan, but neither Ismail nor Soraya would be a candidate since they weren't born in the United States. Even then, sponsorship often took months. Ismail wasn't sure Majida had that long.

"It is with a sad heart that marriage to Fozia is no longer. We divorced."

Ismail stiffened. Divorce among Muslims was rare. To divorce in their homeland, the person seeking the separation only had to say, "I divorce thee," three times, and it was done. But it didn't happen very often since a man was allowed to have more than one wife.

"I am sorry to hear this, Abdul." He knew that Abdul and Fozia's marriage had been arranged by their families, but he assumed that over the years Abdul had grown to love her.

"She will live on third floor with children. And as I am expected, I provide to children and her."

Ismail had been here long enough to know all about divorces in America. They were often very ugly, and no man would ever live in the same house with the woman he was divorcing. But in his home country, a Muslim man was expected to take care of his ex-wife for the rest of his life.

"This is hard news to hear. I wish you the grace of Allah during these troubling times. Did you consider *jirga*?"

Ismail's great-aunt and great-uncle had been part of a jirga when they were having troubles. Ismail was just a young boy at the time, but he still remembered the gathering of the tribal elders to decide the fate of the couple. What he remembered the most was his aunt crying because she was not allowed to divorce his uncle, and the decision of the elders was always final. Years later, his aunt disappeared.

"Fozia and I are to agree that no jirga. Thank you, my cousin, for your nice words. No visa is for Fozia. Rules not allow us in United States."

"Let me think for a moment." Ismail walked back around his desk and sat down again. He'd made a successful career as a urologist, but even he didn't have the kind of money Abdul would need to seek proper care in Pakistan. "Majida is a very sick girl, Abdul. She really needs to come here if she is able. Let me think on this, and I will also talk with my doctor friend who specializes in children with leukemia. Then I will call you."

"In what time is it for call?"

Ismail thought about his trip to Italy. "I will be going on vacation with my fiancée in a couple days, but I will gather as much information as I can before I go." There was a knock at his office door. "I must go now. But I will call you again."

"Mrs. Irvin is here," Erin said as she peeked her head in. "And Mallory needs you to sign a couple of things at the front desk."

Ismail nodded at his nurse, his heart heavy with thoughts

of Majida. The last time he'd seen the child, she was only a year old. "Thank you," he said as he stood up. If Abdul couldn't get a visa to come here, the only option was for him to get her the best medical care he could in Pakistan. A nearly hopeless task.

MALLORY LISTENED AS RHONDA IRVIN TOLD HER HOW much pain she was in. The woman was thirty, only a year older than Mallory, and had given her sister a kidney two months before. Ismail said that she apparently didn't have much tolerance for pain and that the surgery had been very successful for both Rhonda and her sister. Mallory wasn't sure if Ismail was just telling her that because he knew she would one day be a donor in the operating room.

"Oh, Rhonda, I'm so sorry. I'm sure Dr. Fahim will give you something to help with the pain," Mallory said, resting her hand on the frosted window that separated her from the waiting room. "He should be with you shortly, okay?"

Rhonda nodded as Ismail walked up behind Mallory.

"Can you sign these, Dr. Fahim?" she asked. In front of patients she addressed him formally, but he'd insisted that she call him Ismail the rest of the time. His two nurses, Erin and Amber, called him Ismail too. They had been with him for years, and both of them had confirmed what Mallory had thought early on—that Ismail was a wonderful doctor and a very kind man.

After fourteen years in the United States, he still had a hint of a Middle Eastern accent. His close-trimmed facial hair reminded her of Tate's, although Ismail's hair was much shorter and there wasn't a strand out of place. Ismail was smaller than Mallory's muscle-bound boyfriend, but he was a really nice-looking man. They both had that perfect blend of clean-cut with a dash of ruggedness.

The doctor pulled a pen from the pocket of his white coat and scribbled his name in the spots Mallory pointed to. "I see we have a full day today, but when I'm on vacation it will be very quiet here."

Amber would be taking her vacation at the same time. A few patients were scheduled to see Erin for routine follow-ups, and Mallory planned to get caught up on insurance filings. But overall, she was looking forward to a little down time.

Mallory smiled. "We'll see about that."

BY THE TIME SHE GOT TO THE OLIVE GARDEN, MALLORY was pooped. Tate and his mother were waiting for her outside the restaurant. Sweating. July had been brutal, and August was already looking worse.

"So," Regina said after they'd gotten settled at a table and ordered, "Tate said you told your parents that you signed up in the kidney exchange program. Didn't go so well, huh?"

Mallory wasn't sure what Regina's position was on the issue. "No, not really. They feel the same way now as they did when I was seventeen." She paused. "Plus they can't stand the fact that I work for a Muslim. I'd never introduce my parents to Soraya. I'm afraid they'd embarrass me."

They were quiet while the waitress placed salads in front of them. Then Regina reached for Mallory's and Tate's hands.

Tate prayed silently before every meal, which was fine with Mallory, but his mother's out-loud blessings in public made her uncomfortable. She couldn't recall her family ever praying before meals, silently or aloud.

"Amen." Regina let go of their hands and picked up her fork. "You know, Ramadan just ended a few days ago. They don't eat or drink anything during the daylight hours for a month."

Mallory popped an olive into her mouth. "Yeah, I know. Soraya and Ismail are really liberal Muslims, but they do observe Ramadan. And I saw Ismail pulling out his prayer mat more than usual. He usually closes his door, but we've had to interrupt him during prayer a few times."

"I went to a mosque once."

Tate sat taller as he swallowed a piece of bread. "Really, Mom?"

"Yes, I know," Regina said. "It's surprising that this staunch Catholic would do that, but I had a friend who was Muslim. It was before you were born, so it was long before September 11. I'd made a deal with the woman." She paused, frowning. "Good grief, I can't even remember her name. Anyway, I told her I'd go with her to the mosque if she'd attend Mass with me. And she did."

Tate smiled. "Were you trying to convert her?"

Regina shook her head. "Not really. We were both checkers at the grocery store, and we worked the same shift. We became friends and were curious about each other's religion, but neither of us had any interest in converting. I remember a few things about Islam; it's really a very peaceful religion.

Unfortunately, after what happened in New York and the Pentagon, I think most Americans see Muslims in a different light now." Regina got quiet. "I wonder what ever happened to her . . ."

"Well, I'm pretty sure that my parents see them all as terrorists." Mallory sighed.

"The woman I was friends with was a kind and loving person. I can't seem to remember her name, but I do remember that. I haven't thought about her in years."

"Soraya is like that," Mallory said. "Kind and loving. We've gotten to be good friends, and I don't care what God she prays to."

TATE WASN'T SURE IF CHRISTIANS AND MUSLIMS prayed to the same God or not. Or Allah, as they called him. Mallory's casual attitude about the Lord bothered him sometimes, but he wrote it off to the very different ways they were raised. And by the time he and Mallory got back to his place, religious preferences weren't foremost in his thoughts.

She'd followed him home, and they'd barely crossed the threshold of Tate's house when he pulled her into his arms. He cupped her cheeks in his hands and covered her mouth with his, and as she responded, Tate edged them toward his bedroom—and was disappointed when she gently held him at arm's length.

"We need to talk," she said softly.

Tate sighed, never sure what that meant. "Good talk or bad talk?"

Mallory walked to the couch and sat down. She patted the spot beside her. "It's not really good or bad, I don't think. I mean . . . I just think we need to talk about *us* in the event that you get the job in Chicago."

Tate plopped down on the couch and forced a smile. "Okay. Let's talk."

She grinned. "I know you have other things in mind for this evening, but I really think we should talk about this first."

Tate knew Mallory well enough to know that she was probably still analyzing the situation. This conversation was part of the process, and he doubted much would be resolved tonight. Especially since it would all be speculative. "Okay. So you've been thinking about it. What have you come up with?"

She twisted on the couch and tucked one leg beneath her. "Well, first of all, I have a few questions. Number one . . . if you are offered the job, when would they want you to start?"

"I don't know. Les, the guy I know who teaches there, said he doubted they would make a decision before school starts up in a couple of weeks. So it could be that I wouldn't start until after Christmas. They're actually creating the position because they're expanding. It's not like I'm replacing some-one, so I don't think there's a huge sense of urgency."

Mallory tapped a finger to her chin. "Okay, let's just assume you are offered the job."

"Okay." Tate shifted his weight on the couch, eager to hear her thoughts but fearful at the same time.

"You would move to Chicago. I would stay here, and—"

"Wait a minute. I know you love your job, but you

wouldn't move with me? I'm sure there are plenty of jobs for office managers in Chicago, at a doctor's office or anywhere else."

"So my job is less important than yours?"

She smiled, but in Tate's opinion it was one of those thin-lipped smiles women offer up, often in an effort to trip a guy up.

"I didn't say that. But jobs like this for me don't come up very often. I'd be crazy not to jump on it."

She was quiet for a while, and Tate could practically hear the wheels in her head turning.

"I love you, Mallory. If you don't go with me, I won't take the job." His stomach flipped as he said it. *How could I pass this up?*

"Oh no," she said quickly. "Then you would resent me."

"Well, it sounds like you'll resent me if you have to quit your job. So what's the solution?"

They were quiet again. For much longer. Finally, Mallory said, "I'm not relocating with a man I'm not married to."

Oh, thank You, God. Every time he'd hinted to Mallory that he wanted to get married, she'd changed the subject. "Oh, baby." He reached for her hand and squeezed, then brought it to his lips. "I know this isn't the right kind of proposal, but marry me. I didn't think you wanted to get married. Or that you were ready."

The color drained from her face, and Tate was glad he was sitting down.

"That's just it." Her eyes filled with tears. "I'm *not* ready to get married. And I don't know when I will be."

Tate felt the sting of her words, but he willed himself to be calm and took a deep breath. "What does that mean?"

Mallory dabbed at her eye with one finger. "If you get the job in Chicago, Tate, you *have* to take it. I understand how big an opportunity this is. But . . ."

Tate held his breath.

"I won't be going."

ISMAIL FLIPPED THROUGH HIS MAIL WITH HIS CELL phone to his ear. When he heard Soraya opening the door with her key, he told his cousin that he needed to go. He hadn't yet told his fiancée that he had wired Abdul a substantial amount of money to help with Majida's care in Pakistan. Not nearly enough, but all he could spare right now. He hadn't been close to his cousin since they were kids, but Abdul was family and it was Ismail's responsibility to help however he could.

Soraya fell into his arms, and he kissed her gently, then eased her away. "What is the matter, my love? Tell me. What is wrong?"

"Nothing, really," she said as they walked to Ismail's black leather couch. "I'm just tired. It was a long day filled with many customers." Soraya owned a high-end rug shop, and one of her favorites was spread beneath his living room furniture.

She had decorated Ismail's condo, and the woman had a thing for black, white, and red. But somehow it all worked, and even if it didn't he would never say so. The forty-gallon fish tank lent some color to the space. Soraya had filled it with exotic fish, but Ismail forgot to feed them sometimes.

He moved a red throw pillow out of the way as he twisted to face her. Soraya was beautiful inside and out. A silken mass of black hair hung in graceful waves past her shoulders, and her dark eyes were set above high cheekbones against an olive complexion. She looked extra stunning today in a deep purple pantsuit.

After she'd filled him in on her day, he told her about his phone call from Abdul, leaving out the part about the wire transfer.

"Ismail, that makes me so sad." Soraya shook her head. "Is he sure he can't get Majida here for treatment?"

"He says he can't. And I do know it is difficult to get a visa from there to here." He sighed, deciding he didn't want to keep anything from his future wife. "I wired Abdul some money today. Hopefully it will help him find good care for her."

Soraya smiled. "You are a good man."

"I try," he said. He smiled back at her, glad she didn't ask how much.

"Oh, I hired a wedding planner today," she said as she pressed her palms together. "He said eight months isn't long enough to plan the kind of wedding we want, but I explained to him that we are working around Ramadan next July as well as planning two celebrations."

Ismail wished they didn't have to travel so soon after their wedding here, just to have another wedding in Lahore, but it was important to Soraya. "I would think that's plenty of time to plan."

Soraya giggled. "And just how many weddings have you planned?"

Ismail shrugged, grinning. "Not so many." He leaned over and kissed his future wife. "I know it will be wonderful. Both weddings." He briefly thought about the cost of two weddings—thankfully, Soraya's parents were paying for both. Ismail had more money than most, but spending a half million dollars to get married seemed extravagant, even in America. And he wouldn't have been able to send nearly as much to Abdul if he was paying for the weddings.

"I hear your stomach growling." Soraya laid her hand across Ismail's stomach.

"And I'm happy that fasting is over."

She gave his stomach a gentle pat. "Fasting has been written down upon you as it was upon those before you."

"Yes, yes," he said. Soraya came from a very liberal Muslim family in Lahore, but she could cite the Quran better than most people. "Stay with me tonight," he whispered as he leaned forward and kissed her.

She didn't answer as she got up off the couch and rounded the corner. Ismail heard the bathroom door close, then listened to his stomach growl some more. During the past month of Ramadan, he wasn't sure which had been more difficult—abstaining from food during the daylight hours or abstaining from Soraya in the nights. Ismail knew they weren't the best Muslims in the world, and they seldom went to the mosque. But they did practice the call to prayer five times per day, and they did abstain from things that would be displeasing to Allah during Ramadan.

Despite the rumbling in his belly, when Soraya came back into the room in a flowing black dressing gown, he was clear about his priorities. The phone vibrating in his pocket was an unwelcome distraction, but he was a doctor, so he pulled it out and checked the caller ID. He quickly pressed Ignore, stood up, and walked toward his beautiful Soraya, with no plans to return his father's call. The man still terrified him. Even from across the world.

Chapter Four

Mallory scribbled in the code on the insurance claim before she picked up the phone.

"Dr. Fahim's office. May I help you?"

Silence for a few moments. "Hello. Who is speaking?" The caller spoke with a thick accent.

"This is Mallory. Dr. Fahim is out of the office. May I help you with something or take a message?"

"Hello, Mallory. I hope this day that you are good."

In truth, she wasn't; her heart was heavy with thoughts of Tate, whom she hadn't spoken to in three days. But she responded politely, "My day is good. Thank you."

"I phone Ismail at his portable phone many times. I know he is at a holiday in Italy. Please ask for his call to me. I am Abdul."

Mallory slid the message pad in front of her and picked up her pen, doubtful Ismail would return any nonemergency calls until he and Soraya returned from vacation. "And what is your number, Mr. Abdul?"

"He has number. Only Abdul. I am cousin to Ismail."

"Oh. Okay." Ismail never talked about his family. Soraya said it was painful for him to talk about his childhood. "I'm not sure when I'll hear from him, but I will be sure to give him the message."

After she hung up, she returned to the pile of claims. Whatever it took to stay busy and not think about the blowup with Tate. When she'd told him she wouldn't move to Chicago with him, he'd actually cried. They'd both agreed to take a few days to think about things. So she had, until late into the nights.

She knew Tate was right. She could find another job in Chicago. And she could still stay in the kidney exchange program in the Windy City, make a difference, save a life. And she would be with Tate. Problem was . . . she didn't want to do any of that. She was born in Houston. Her life was here. Despite their dysfunction, her family was here. Even though a lot of her friends were married, had children, and had shifted their interests, this was still where she wanted to be. She found herself having the most awful thoughts—actually wishing that Tate wouldn't get the job so nothing would have to change. *So selfish of me.*

She glanced at her cell phone. Not even a text.

TATE CALCULATED HIS ROUTE FROM HOUSTON TO Chicago on his laptop. A seventeen-hour drive. As much as he wanted this job, it was hard to be excited with things the way they were with Mallory. He picked up his cell phone and sent her a text: I MISS YOU. I LOVE YOU. LEAVING FOR CHICAGO TOMORROW A.M. A few minutes later, his phone rang.

"I miss you too," she said when he answered. "And I love you. No matter where each of us is, that will never change."

Tate closed his eyes for a few seconds and smiled. "Do you want to ride with me to Chicago? Can you take off?"

"No. Ismail and Soraya are in Italy for ten days, remember? Amber is on vacation, too, so even if it wasn't such short notice, I can't leave Erin here by herself."

"Oh yeah. I remember now."

"Are you sure you don't want to fly?"

Tate set his laptop beside him on the couch. No one wished he could fly more than Tate. He dreaded the long drive.

"No, I'll stop somewhere along the way and spend the night, then make the rest of the trip the next day." He had come close to buying a plane ticket in the past. He figured he might get as far as the gate, but he was sure he wouldn't actually be able to board the aircraft. He shivered just thinking about it.

"Do you think they'll make an offer while you're there?"

"I don't know. I'm meeting with the committee." He was tempted to beg her to come over tonight, but he wanted to be fresh for the trip. As much as he'd missed her, he was worried they would stay up too late—or worse, get into another fight.

"What about ET? Is your neighbor going to feed him?"

Tate stood up. "Yeah, but thanks for the reminder. I need to put the key in the usual hiding spot." He grabbed the extra key from a drawer in the kitchen and put it outside.

"Do you want to come over tonight? I can make us dinner."

Tate could hear in her voice that she really had missed him. "I think I better stay home. I gotta get up really early or I'd ask you to come here."

They were quiet for a while.

Mallory cleared her throat. "Okay, well . . . I guess I'll let you go."

Her words seemed a bit clipped. "Are you mad?"

"Nope."

"Okay. I'll call you when I get there."

"Great. Have a safe trip. And good luck with everything."

Confirmed. She was mad that he didn't want to see her tonight. He could give in or just ride out the conversation. He chose the latter. "I love you."

"I love you too."

After they hung up, Tate picked up his laptop again. But he couldn't shake the feeling that his relationship with Mallory was headed in a bad direction.

ISMAIL UNPACKED HIS SUITCASE, SOMETHING HE DID only when he was traveling with Soraya. She liked everything put away in the drawers of the hotel, shoes lined up in the closet, toiletries put in easy access locations in the bathroom, and everything hung in the closet. As usual, one of her first phone calls was to the maître d' to request more hangers. And that was all okay with Ismail. He was a blessed man to have her and not about to complain.

"You missed a call on your cell phone," she said as she hung a blue dress in the closet. "I heard it ringing when you were in the bathroom."

Ismail stashed the last of his clothes in the bottom drawer. "Yeah, I heard it." He walked to the nightstand where he'd laid his cell phone and picked it up. "It was my father." Dropping the phone on the bed, he walked to the window, pleased with the view of the Amalfi Coast he'd requested. He'd never been to Positano, but he could already see why it was one of Soraya's favorite places. The picturesque town was perched on the enclave of a hill and wound down to the water, connecting everything with flights of stairs. It surely wasn't a place to visit if you didn't like walking. Ismail considered himself to be in pretty good shape, but he'd been winded after walking up the stairs that seemed to go on forever. Even Soraya, who was in better shape than he was, had to stop a couple of times to rest. But the view from the top was breathtaking.

"Do you need to call him back?" Soraya retrieved another dress from her suitcase and walked back to the closet.

"Maybe later." He opened the sliding glass door and breathed in the fresh air, then walked out onto the patio. There was always a purpose to his father's calls. And it was never good. Just the sound of the man's voice brought forth memories that still plagued Ismail all these years later.

Soraya joined him on the patio, having changed from her

traveling clothes. She looked beautiful in anything, but she was even lovelier in a flowery, flowing dress that hung just below her knees. And her cute little feet, toenails painted a bright red, were enclosed in a pair of strappy sandals the same color. Even Ismail knew that painted toes and fingers weren't allowed in Islam, but his Soraya chose to break the rules from time to time. She cuddled up next to him and kissed him on the cheek.

"Thank you for bringing me here."

Ismail pulled her close. Soraya had led a privileged life, having traveled during much of her growing-up years, but she never flaunted it. She had loving, wonderful parents who just happened to have a lot of money. But it was hard to believe that he and Soraya had grown up in the same country, such different lives they'd led.

"It is a beautiful place." Ismail stared out across the bluest water he'd ever seen and felt the refreshing breeze in his face.

He and Soraya had done their share of traveling together, but this was their first time outside of the United States. Ismail was always afraid he'd be pulled aside at the airport and sent back home. There was no reason for him to be deported, and he'd never done anything illegal in his life, but the thought was always there. Going back to his homeland would be a fate worse than death. He'd never admitted his fears to Soraya because he knew they were unfounded. When she'd asked him at the airport why he was so nervous, he told her he was anxious about the long flight.

"Are you hungry?" Soraya tucked her dark hair behind her ears.

"I am a little hungry." He turned to her and pushed back the shorter strands of her hair that were swept to one side above her eyebrow. The woman had no idea how beautiful she was. "Are you?"

She rose up on her tiptoes, kissed him tenderly on the mouth, and smiled. "Yes. Let's eat."

Ismail felt a hunger pang that had nothing to do with food, but he nodded.

Soraya grabbed his hand, and they walked back into their room. "There is a place near here where I've eaten before. It's outstanding." She frowned. "Are you sure you don't want to call your father back first? What if it's an emergency?"

Ismail shrugged. "Everything is an emergency to him."

Right then his phone started ringing and buzzing on the nightstand.

"Talk to him so he doesn't keep calling. I'll go down to the spa and make us appointments for tomorrow." She blew him a kiss before she left.

"Hello, Father." Ismail sat down on the bed.

"Ismail. Finally, I reach you." His father spoke fairly good English. "You were told of Majida's sickness by Abdul."

"Yes, Father." Ismail should have known his father would be calling about this. Maybe he'd worried unnecessarily. "I was hoping to get Majida to the United States, but Abdul said they can't get visas." He wasn't going to tell his father that he'd sent money to Abdul. It would make his cousin look dishonorable, even though the money was for his daughter.

"Yes. This is my understanding. Abdul has a few scratches

in his past that prevent him from obtaining a visa to your country."

Abdul hadn't mentioned any "scratches" when he'd given Ismail reasons he couldn't get a visa. Ismail realized he didn't know his cousin anymore.

It was unfortunate, but over the years, Ismail had grown to distrust many of his own people. He could remember exactly where he was when the Twin Towers were hit in New York City and the overwhelming sadness he'd felt. He'd never felt more American in his life as he sat in the coffee shop near his office and watched the scene unfold on the television screen. And for the first time, Ismail had been ashamed to be Muslim.

He had been in America barely a year, but he could still recall the way his new American friends walked away from him, as if he were one of the pilots flying one of the planes on that fateful day. It was an old wound that he thought had healed, but it would reopen from time to time—especially when he got on an airplane and he could see the fear in other passengers' eyes. He wanted to stand up and scream, "I am one of you. I am an American!" He'd been fortunate to have found some wonderful American friends. And of course he'd found Soraya.

"What kind of scratches?" he asked.

"Small things, not of importance. Only important is that we must get Abdul and Majida to the United States so that she will be cared for."

Ismail raised his shoulders and dropped them slowly. "Father, I've done everything I know to do. I cannot sponsor

Abdul because I wasn't born in the United States. And even if Abdul was to obtain visas through sponsorship, that takes months. I worry that Majida might not have that long. He needs to seek treatment for Majida right away, in Pakistan."

Ismail closed his eyes as he fought to push aside memories, recollections that assaulted him every time he talked to his father. The beatings had left plenty of scars, but it was always his brother's face at the forefront of all the horrors.

"There is a way for Abdul to take Majida to your United States." Shahid Fahim spat out *United States* as if just saying the words left a bitter taste in his mouth. Ismail didn't know anyone who hated Americans more than his father. "Abdul needs an American wife. That will expedite his travels with his sick daughter."

"You're probably right. If Abdul was married to an American, the authorities might overlook some of those 'scratches' so he could get help for his daughter."

"Then you find him one. A wife."

"What?" Ismail stood up and paced the room. "I don't know anyone who would go to Pakistan. Father, it's very dangerous for Americans there."

"You will find someone." His father rattled off a string of curses at Ismail, then said, "Do you want Majida to die? Is that what you want? Have you no honor, enough to help your own family?"

"Of course I don't want her to die." He reminded himself that his father was far away, that he wasn't going to come storming into the room any moment. "But I don't know any American who would do this." *Nor would I recommend it to anyone.*

His father cursed at him some more, then hung up.

Ismail sat on the edge of the bed trembling. Remembering. It was amazing that the man could still have this effect on him all these years later.

He reached into his back pocket and pulled out his wallet. He found Faisal's picture, the only photo Ismail had of his only sibling. Faisal was the reason Ismail had sought refuge in the United States. The reason he'd worked so hard to go to college. And definitely the reason he'd chosen urology as his occupation.

CHAPTER FIVE

The August sun shone through the glass windows behind Ismail's desk, where he sat quietly as Mallory wept. He'd waited until the last Saturday morning patient left and the nurses, too, had gone home.

"I'm so sorry, Mallory."

"I just can't believe it."

Ismail sighed. "The world needs more people like you who are willing to be a live donor. But impaired glucose tolerance is a prediabetic condition that disqualifies you." He handed her a tissue across the desk.

Mallory sniffled, then dabbed at her eyes with the tissue. "I don't understand. What does prediabetic even mean? I'm not sick."

"No, but it means we'll need to be monitoring your glucose levels to be sure it doesn't progress. Right now all you need to do is exercise more and limit your sugar intake—good ideas for all of us."

"Well, my parents will be thrilled. Tate will be happy too."

Ismail leaned back in his chair. "I know this was important to you. But it must not be in Allah's plan for your life."

Then what exactly is God's plan for me? Everyone around her seemed to credit God for His fabulous plans. She blew her nose and took a deep breath.

"I promised my cousin that even though I couldn't save her life, I was going to save someone. It's number one on my bucket list." She looked away. "But apparently it's not going to happen."

"Maybe you should have been a doctor." Ismail spoke softly as he offered her a gentle smile. "For me, becoming a urologist was very personal."

Mallory waited, wondering if he was going to explain. "I actually considered it," she said. "But I didn't have the grades."

Ismail stood up. "I know that we have dinner plans with you and Tate tonight. If you'd like to postpone, I know that Soraya will understand."

"No, I'll be okay. I'm just shocked." She'd get through it for Soraya's sake. It had taken a long time to get their four schedules to jibe. "I should have made plans to donate a kidney a long time ago. Things kept getting in the way. And my parents are so opposed." She shrugged. "I guess I'll just have to find another way to save a life."

She stood up, and when Ismail walked around to where she was standing, he put a gentle hand on her arm.

"Sometimes when Allah shuts one door, he opens another."

ISMAIL AND SORAYA WERE ALREADY SEATED WHEN Mallory and Tate got there. Soraya stood up and hugged Mallory. "Ismail gave me your news, and I am so sorry."

"I'm okay." Mallory forced a smile, then she and Tate sat down. Tate reached for her hand and squeezed three times. She squeezed back. *I love you too.*

After introductions were made and wine was ordered, Soraya and Mallory started wedding talk, while Ismail and Tate found a common interest in baseball. Mallory did her best to stay focused.

"Good thing we made reservations," Soraya said as she glanced around. Every table was full, but all the patrons had the same amazing view. After a thirty-four-story ride in a glass-enclosed elevator, they were seated next to a glass wall in the revolving restaurant that overlooked the city.

"This is a very cool place," Tate said.

"I read that it takes forty-five minutes for it to go all the way around," Mallory said.

"The food is excellent too." Soraya lowered her menu. "I suppose it's a Houston landmark." She smiled. "So glad we could finally all get together."

Tate looked amazing this evening in tan slacks, a crisp blue shirt, and a sports jacket. Mallory had chosen sleek black leggings, dressy heels, and a silver tunic. In her opinion, though, she was never going to look as good as her friend, who was wearing a fitted red dress with tiny black dots on it.

Tate had never eaten at the Spindletop before, and she

knew he was worried about how much it was going to cost. When Soraya ordered a two-hundred-dollar bottle of wine, he went a little pale.

Mallory stared at her menu. Nothing sounded very good at the moment, but she finally settled on the seared snapper with crawfish spinach béchamel and butternut squash risotto.

When the waiter came up to tell them about the special and take their orders, Ismail ordered for himself and Soraya. Mallory wondered if he always ordered for his fiancée. Did he just know what she liked, or did he make the decisions for both of them?

"Thank you, my darling," Soraya said after the waiter left.

"You are welcome, my princess." Ismail kissed her on the cheek. He turned to the others. "Did you know that Soraya was named after a queen?"

Mallory swallowed a bite of bread. "No, I didn't. The queen of Pakistan?"

"She was queen of Afghanistan and the first Muslim consort who appeared with her husband in public," Soraya replied. "Completely unheard of in the twenties. She was a great woman, instrumental in enforcing change for women."

"Well, my love . . ." Ismail smiled. "*You* are my queen."

Soraya winked at him but then went on. "Queen Tarzi encouraged women to get an education, and her husband often campaigned against the veil. She once ripped off her veil in public after one of her husband's speeches."

"Why *do* women wear the veil?" asked Mallory. "And how come you don't have to?" She'd done some reading about it but had been hoping for a chance to ask Soraya.

"Like so many religious beliefs, it depends on where you live and how you were raised. And how different people interpret the Quran. My mother chooses to wear the *hijab* in public and when she is around men who are not relatives. My sister, on the other hand, doesn't wear it at all."

"So when you go home, do you cover your head?"

"It depends on the situation and who I will be around." Soraya tucked a strand of dark hair behind her ear. "Muslim women are constantly defending their choice to cover themselves, but the truth is, we see it as a symbol of piety and a sign of inner strength and fortitude. But having said that, I am a Muslim woman living in America, so I choose not to cover myself."

Mallory nodded. Despite her beauty and designer clothes, Soraya never wore anything too low-cut or revealing. The woman was a class act, for sure—no matter what religion she practiced. Mallory glanced at Tate and, to her embarrassment, saw that he was checking something on his cell phone. Then she looked at Ismail, and he was also fumbling with his phone.

Soraya elbowed Ismail, then pointed to Tate. "Look at the two of you. If I didn't know better, I'd think we were boring you boys."

But Tate's expression was tight and strained, his lips pressed firmly together. "Excuse me, please." He put his napkin on the table, pushed back his chair, and glanced around the room.

"The little boys' room is that way." Soraya pointed to her right, and Tate hurried away.

TATE WALKED INTO THE MEN'S ROOM AND REREAD THE e-mail from Les. He'd been waiting over a week, trying not to be anxious but thinking about little else but the job . . . and Mallory.

> Hi Tate,
>
> I hope this e-mail finds you well. You'll be getting a formal letter from the committee, of course, but I wanted you to hear first from me. I'm sorry to report that they have chosen someone else to fill the new position. I know this isn't the news you hoped for. Basically, it was down to you and one other guy, and the other guy had a lot more teaching experience.
>
> You're a talented musician and a wonderful teacher, and I know the perfect opportunity will present itself. I am keeping my eyes and ears open, my friend.
>
> Best regards,
> Les

Tate didn't think he realized until this moment exactly how much he'd wanted this job. He took care of business, washed his hands, then just stood there. Should he go back to the group and announce that Mallory wouldn't have to worry about quitting her job? After a few moments he decided not to say anything. He'd wait and tell her when they got in the car. On the way back to the table, he thought about all the things he had done wrong or omitted during the interview. And why hadn't he played something more challenging for them, like Chopin's "Fantaisie Impromptu"?

When he got back to the table, the appetizers were there, but the crab cakes weren't looking too good anymore.

Mallory and Ismail were talking about someone named Abdul, and Soraya was the one fiddling with her phone now. He noticed the giant rock on her ring finger. He would never be able to afford something like that, assuming Mallory ever agreed to marry him.

"I don't mind helping your cousin," Mallory said. "Some of those forms are hard to fill out even when you speak good English." She shook her head. "And that is just awful about his daughter."

Ismail looked sad. "It really is. Thank you for helping him. I'm going to send him your e-mail address, if that's okay." Mallory nodded. "It's an application for aid, and the company is based in the United States."

Tate picked at the crab, wishing he could get up and go home. The need to be alone was overwhelming. Mallory probably felt the same way. They should have rescheduled this dinner.

Soraya dropped her phone back in her purse, then hung the bag on her chair. "So, Tate, I have something to ask you." She glanced at Ismail and smiled, then looked back at Tate. "You and Mallory will be our guests at the wedding here in Houston, of course. But I was wondering if you would also like to play the piano for a while for our guests, perhaps as people

BETH WISEMAN

are coming in and getting settled? We have this in the budget, but we haven't chosen anyone. And Mallory tells me that you are the best piano player in the world."

Tate forced a smile. "I don't know about that." *And certainly not when pitted against others in the business.* He tried not to let the bitterness creep into his voice. "But I'd be happy to play for your guests." He'd done that type of gig plenty of times. What was one more wedding?

Soraya gently clapped her hands together. "Yes, yes. It should be grand. I was thinking maybe you could play for an hour." She turned to Ismail. "My love, what do you think?"

Ismail nodded. "It's your show, Princess."

"Yes, it is," she said as she winked at her fiancé.

Tate struggled through the rest of the meal, commenting when appropriate, and grateful when Ismail picked up the tab.

THEY'D ONLY BEEN IN THE CAR A FEW MINUTES WHEN Mallory turned down the radio and looked toward him. "So, are you going to tell me what's wrong? It's not like you to turn down dessert."

"I didn't get the job in Chicago. I got an e-mail from Les while we were at dinner."

Mallory was quiet. "I'm sorry, Tate. I really am."

"Life goes on," he said as he looked at her.

Even in the darkness, it resembled more of a glare. But she was pretty sure her bad news today trumped his. Just the same, she would try to tread lightly.

50

"It probably just means that a better opportunity is down the road. That just wasn't the right job." She reached into her purse, checked her own e-mail, and saw she had one from . . . Abdul. She opened it.

My dear Mallory,

It is with fond heart that I ask for your help. Ismail sends to me your e-mail code, and I take this time to tell you of Majida. The look of it is not good. Doctor says six months for life. We do not tell Majida this news. Ismail says hospital at Lahore is only hope for wellness. Many forms. One in English.

I send you peace and blessings.

Abdul

Mallory opened the attachment and was familiar with the company. "I just got an e-mail from Ismail's cousin, the one he was talking about at dinner. The doctor says his daughter only has six months to live." She paused, shaking her head. "I just can't even imagine." Her news had been a blow, but this was life or death for this girl.

Tate didn't say anything.

"Anyway, it's just too bad that he can't get her here, to Houston. I bet that six months could turn into a lot longer if she was at MD Anderson or Texas Children's."

Tate stayed quiet but laid on the horn when a car pulled out in front of him. He turned the radio up. Mallory turned it back down.

"Tate, I know you're upset about the job in Chicago, but

you need to keep things in perspective. We both got some bad news today." She steadied herself on the dash when Tate made a really sharp turn. "But we aren't dying."

Tate turned the radio up again, and Mallory knew she should just be quiet. But she and Tate had a lot to be thankful for. "It's just a job."

"Well, it wasn't just a job to me. Opportunities at that type of school don't come along very often."

Mallory sat quietly, biting her lip, with a clear understanding about how the rest of the evening was going to go if they didn't both change their attitudes. And Mallory was pretty sure Tate should be comforting her. She pushed forward anyway. "Did you like the Spindletop?"

"It was okay."

"I thought it was great. And it was nice of Ismail to pick up the tab. And how cool is it that they want you to play at their wedding dinner? Soraya told me that two senators will be there, and . . . are you ready for this? Her wedding gown cost forty-eight thousand dollars!"

Tate grunted. "And she had to brag about that to you? Seems in poor taste."

—"She didn't tell me the cost. She showed me a picture and told me the designer name, and I Googled it. She's just an excited bride who wanted to show me a picture of her wedding dress."

"Why aren't they having a Muslim wedding? Since that's what they are."

Mallory understood that Tate was upset, but this was

veering way out of character for him. She took a deep breath. "They're having another ceremony in Lahore two months later."

"Oh. Two weddings. Does she have another forty-eight-thousand-dollar dress, or heaven forbid, would she wear the same one?"

"You know what, Tate? I understand that you're upset, but you don't have to be so ugly."

He took his hands off the wheel and lifted them in the air. "What's so ugly about asking if your new friend will have two wedding dresses? Two weddings. Seems likely that she'd have two dresses."

"I think the other wedding will be a Muslim ceremony." She stared straight ahead, chewing on her bottom lip.

"They don't seem like real Muslims to me. Otherwise, they'd dress like their people." Tate turned onto Mallory's street.

"Maybe you're not a real Catholic either. It's not about what people wear."

He pulled into the parking lot of her apartment. "That's a dumb thing to say. It *is* about what they wear to them. And I don't understand how Ismail and Soraya can walk among us like they're no different if they really believe in Islam. It's almost like they're fakes or something."

Mallory opened the door, fairly sure that Tate wasn't coming up to her place. And that was just fine. "I'll just talk to you later, Tate, when you're not being such a jerk." She got out of the car and slammed the door. He actually squealed his tires when he left.

BETH WISEMAN

Mallory was shaking as she unlocked her front door. She allowed herself an hour to cry. The type of sobs she wouldn't want anyone to see or hear. Twice she reminded herself she was in an apartment and she'd have to keep her wailing down. But when she was done, in her jammies and tucked into bed, she pulled her computer onto her lap. Her head was spinning, and she knew sleep wasn't going to come for a while. Normally, she'd call Tate. Not tonight. She thought about a man across the world who had just learned that his sixteen-year-old daughter had only months to live if they didn't get help soon. She logged into her e-mail and decided to write back to Abdul. Someone with a far larger problem than either she or Tate had.

CHAPTER SIX

Ismail opened the door to his condo and stepped aside for Soraya. She slipped off her heels by the front door and wiggled her toes before she walked to the couch and sat down. Ismail got out of his jacket, tossed it on one of the chairs, and joined her.

"It was a great meal." He yawned, hoping it would be time for sleep soon.

She twisted to face him. "So, what did you think of Tate?"

Ismail shrugged. "He was okay."

"I liked him very much. And he is a handsome fellow." She pinched him gently on the cheek. "But of course, he is not as handsome as my Ismail."

"I noticed he didn't even reach for the bill. I mean . . . I planned to pay for it since Mallory is my employee, but still." He paused as he thought about the evening. "I don't think he's good enough for Mallory."

Soraya laughed. "Now, Ismail. You haven't even known Mallory very long. How can you possibly say that? I thought Tate was wonderful."

Ismail shrugged. "I thought he was a little . . . boring." In truth, Ismail liked Tate. But he didn't *want* to like a man whose life he was playing with.

She slapped him gently on the arm. "Ismail. That is not true. I didn't find him to be boring at all. Maybe he just didn't have time to get a word in edgewise with the rest of us talking. Or maybe he's a little shy. Either way, I think he's delightful."

That was his Soraya, always finding the best in everyone. The woman never met a stranger, and everyone loved her. But no one could possibly love her as much as he did.

"I'm off to the shower."

Ismail nodded, and once he heard the water running, he dialed his father's number. They'd had several conversations today. Ismail was hoping this would be the last one for a while.

"The ball is rolling," he said after his father answered.

"You found someone to marry your cousin?"

"Maybe. I've put him in contact with someone, but the rest is up to Abdul."

He'd been trying to justify his actions all day long. But Mallory wanted to save a life. And Abdul needed an American wife so he could save his daughter's life. It was a win-win for everyone if his cousin could woo Mallory to go to Pakistan and marry him in name only. And the timing seemed right. Soraya had told him that Mallory was upset with Tate about a possible move to Chicago. Once Abdul had brought Majida to the United States for treatment of her cancer, Mallory could divorce him.

Ismail hated that his father still had this kind of manipulative power over him. But Shahid Fahim had mentioned Soraya's name one too many times since their first conversation about finding Abdul an American wife. There wasn't an outright threat, but the implication was clear. *Find your cousin a wife, or Soraya could be in danger.*

As bad as he felt about his involvement, Ismail knew that if there had to be a sacrifice, it would have to be Mallory. He knew what his father was capable of. He'd sold his brother's kidney on the black market for money when Faisal was fourteen. Ismail could still remember how terrified Faisal was. And ultimately, with no post care, his brother had died. Now Ismail sent money monthly to an organization in Pakistan that worked to prevent underground organ transplants.

But Abdul had his work cut out for him. Peshawar was in the tribal belt of Pakistan. If Mallory had any sense at all, she'd know it was one of the most dangerous places in the world—especially for an American—and she wouldn't even consider a trip there.

MALLORY IGNORED THE VIBRATING CELL PHONE NEXT to her on the bed. She was enjoying her e-mails with Abdul, and Tate could just wait until the morning to hear from her. Besides, she and Abdul had decided to Skype, and she was waiting for his call to come through. Mallory had seen Tate using the video communication software when he talked to his cousin in Virginia. Amazing that you could see someone right on your computer screen and have a conversation.

She lay on her stomach on her bed, propped her elbows in front of her, and cupped her cheeks with her hands as she stared at the screen. She glanced at the clock, thankful that tomorrow was Sunday and she could sleep in. It was the middle of the day, though, for her new friend. Abdul had talked to her via e-mail about his daughter. About his fears and worries. His biggest concern was finding good health care for Majida. Abdul worked at a bank, but he said he didn't have health insurance, so money was an issue. He sounded like a wonderful father, and about an hour into the e-mails, Mallory told him about her cousin Kelsey and how she'd learned today that she wouldn't be able to be a kidney donor. He'd been so kind and sympathetic. She jumped when the call came through, and it took a few seconds for Abdul to come into focus.

"My dear Mallory, how good to *see* you." Abdul's voice came through the computer speaker loud and clear. She liked the way he had started each e-mail with, "My dear Mallory." He smiled, blinking his eyes a few times. "You are most beautiful."

So are you. Mallory couldn't believe how handsome this man was, like Ismail, even though they didn't look anything alike. Mallory was expecting a swarthy older man, probably wearing a turban on his head. This guy looked to be in his late thirties and had kind, dark eyes, black hair, a neatly trimmed goatee, and an amazing smile. He was wearing a white shirt buttoned to his neck. Apparently Ismail and Abdul were both blessed with the handsome gene. She'd been needing a distraction, and Abdul would certainly do. She felt herself blushing even though the man was on the other side of the world.

"Thank you," she finally said. "It's good to see you too."

"I overflow with wonder at such beauty."

A warm and welcome glow flowed through her at the sound of his voice. "You're very kind. Thank you again."

"I enjoy starting to know you. How does beautiful woman like you have no husband or children? Are you not of age for this?"

"Uh . . . yes, I am of age." She paused as she latched onto a strand of hair and twirled it around her finger. She opted not to tell Abdul that she couldn't have children. "I do have a boyfriend though."

Abdul nodded. There was a slight delay on Skype, but overall she could see him quite clearly.

"He will marry you then?"

Her "distraction" was treading into waters Mallory didn't want to wade in. She coughed, clearing her throat. "I think that we'll get married someday."

Abdul grinned. "Be good for him to hurry before another takes someone so lovely for wife."

"Abdul, you really are very kind." Mallory was realizing what a rut she and Tate had fallen into after four years together. She could recall a time when Tate was this adoring. She saw a woman's hand slide a cup of coffee in front of Abdul, along with a small plate of something that looked like cookies. "Is that your wife?"

"She is my before wife. 'Ex-wife,' you say."

Mallory wondered what his ex-wife was doing bringing him coffee and cookies.

Abdul took a sip from the cup. "Fozia still brings tea and biscuits to me each day. Fozia and my children live on third floor. I stay on number two floor."

Mallory's eyes widened. "You and your ex-wife live in the same house?"

Abdul raised his chin slightly but smiled. "Yes. Of course. It is my job for taking care of Fozia and my children always, no matter if we divorce."

"Really?" Mallory blinked her eyes a couple of times. "Hmm . . ." She thought about her sister's divorce from Nelson and what a war zone it had been.

Abdul lifted an eyebrow, grinning. Mallory smiled back at him, still surprised at how handsome he was—though she didn't know why she should be.

"Is it not the job for a husband to take care of his family in your country?" Abdul reached for a cookie but just held it as he waited for Mallory to respond.

"I guess you could say that it is the husband's job to help support the children financially after a divorce, but in most cases he wouldn't be required to take care of the wife." She wondered if Abdul understood all this, but she went on. "It would be unheard of for the husband and wife to still live in the same house after they're divorced." She paused. "Can you understand my English?"

Abdul was still holding the cookie, frowning. "I don't know if understanding. Man does not take care of family for lifetime?"

Mallory shook her head. "No. He will help support the children until they go off to college, sometimes through college, but he has no responsibility to take care of the wife. Sometimes he is required to give her money, if they had a prior agreement before they got married. And in some states there is alimony, which is an amount the man pays to the woman because maybe she never worked, or for other reasons." She paused, shrugging. "But most of the time, no spousal support."

Abdul narrowed his eyebrows as he put the cookie back on the plate. "How will wife who is no more eat? What would she do?"

Mallory gave another slight shrug. "In most cases, the ex-wife would work. Some don't, if they have a lot of money."

Abdul shook his head. "There is no honor in that. Women are treasure, even if not good marriage. It is man's job to provide and care for her. Forever."

"Really?" Mallory had read enough to know that women didn't have a lot of rights there, and she didn't think they were treated very well either. She decided to test her new friend. "What if your wife—or ex-wife—wanted to work, would she be allowed to?"

Abdul smiled as he leaned back in his chair. "Why would she want work when I will give care to her?"

Mallory knew she would work, even if her husband was a millionaire. She thought about Tate. Chances were he'd never have a ton of money, and Mallory couldn't care less. "Even . . ." She grinned. "Even if my husband wanted to take care of me, I would still want to work, to keep my mind sharp, to learn new things, and . . . so I didn't get bored."

Abdul nodded. "There are some ladies whose thoughts are like yours. And it is accepted."

Her new friend seemed willing to talk about anything, so she took a step further out of the box. "What do most people in your country think of Americans?"

Abdul's face went solemn. "Much like you think of people in my country. You know not who to trust. Many terrorists in Northwest Territory. Home to the former Bin Laden. I think you mostly think we are all terrorists." He paused. "But we are as afraid of Americans as you are of us. Who to trust? Your mechanic planes with no people bomb our villages, killing children and those who have no war with you."

"Drones." Mallory didn't care for the drones either. Although her father had a completely different opinion and saw the air strikes as necessary. Mallory knew it was an effort to kill the bad guys, but so many innocent lives were lost in the process.

Abdul had mentioned in an e-mail that he also had two boys.

"Tell me about your other children, your two sons."

His face brightened. "Yes. My boys are Waleed at twelve years old. Zyiad is ten. And you've already heard about my beloved Majida. A beautiful girl. Like you."

Abdul complimented so freely, and it made Mallory smile again along with him.

"Children are a gift from Allah." Abdul's eyes gleamed as he spoke.

Tate's mother always said that too—that children were a gift from God.

Allah? God? Mallory wondered sometimes . . . if she'd had Jewish parents, she would have been raised in a Jewish household. If her parents were Mormon, she'd be a Mormon. In Abdul's country, she'd be practicing Islam. How could some people believe they were the only ones going to heaven when they could have just as easily had different beliefs if they had been born somewhere else? Was this part of God's plan? To have some people just be born into a family, doomed to burn in hell because they were taught to believe a certain way? And which group was correct? Or were they all wrong?

"Do you believe that Christians will go to heaven?" Mallory held her breath. It was a random question, but before her friendship with this man grew, it was something she wanted to know.

His dark eyes were hooded like a hawk's, and for a moment he studied her intently. "I believe good Christians will go to paradise." His eyebrows narrowed. "Why do you ask?"

She could feel her face turning red. "I don't know. I guess I just wondered."

"Not all my people believe that those not Islam will go to paradise. Some believe that if not Islam, you will forever be in hell." He paused. "Me . . . I believe that those of the Book will share time in paradise."

"Those of the book?"

He nodded. "Muslims, Christians, Jews . . . yes." Frowning, he shook his head. "Hindu, Buddhist, or nonbelievers . . . no. They will go to hell."

Mallory swallowed hard, thinking that was rather harsh, but she wasn't enough of a theologian to argue. "Most

Christians believe that you have to accept Jesus as your Lord and Savior to get to heaven, and that anyone who doesn't will burn in hell."

He studied her face from the other side of the world, yet only a couple of feet from her. "And what do you believe, my dear Mallory?"

Mallory was wondering if she should have started this conversation. What little she knew about Islam didn't really qualify her to get into a theological discussion with a man she didn't know. "Well . . ." She paused and took a deep breath. "My boyfriend is Catholic, and he would disagree with what I'm about to say, but I believe that Jesus died on the cross for us, making a place for us in heaven. But—unlike my boyfriend, Tate—I also think that God will take a good hard look at the lives we've lived here on earth. To some extent, I believe that we are responsible for the choices we make. But, like I said, a lot of Christians don't feel this way."

Abdul ran a finger back and forth across the short, dark stubble on his chin, and for a long while he just stared at her as if he were assessing her comments.

Then the screen went blank, and he was gone. Mallory wasn't sure if she'd crossed a line with her questions or if the power had gone off, which he had warned her happened a lot. It took about fifteen minutes before he called back, citing a power outage. But their conversation veered away from religion, and Mallory figured that was probably good.

Her eyes were heavy, but she wasn't ready to stop talking to him. His passion for life, love for his family, and incredible faith made him even more attractive than his physical beauty.

She asked him how long he had been married to his wife, and he freely shared about his marriage of eighteen years and subsequent divorce.

"So, I marry her with hope to love her." Abdul smiled after telling Mallory about his arranged marriage to Fozia. "And I did fall happily in love with her. But we be not souls united by Allah. Did not feel perfect from beginning. Now, better we stay apart." He paused, smiling. "You, my dear Mallory, are most beautiful woman. Your heart pulls to my heart. Your soul touches mine."

She was so angry with Tate that it was easy to fall under Abdul's spell. Even with all of the man's troubles and worries about Majida, he was reaching out to her in a way that she needed right now. They had shared a lot with each other in a short time, and in some ways it seemed so incredibly safe. But on a totally different level, there was an air of mystery about Abdul, an edginess that made him interesting, exciting.

"I'm enjoying getting to know you too, Abdul. I've really enjoyed talking this evening." She glanced at the clock on her laptop and stifled a yawn.

He kept his eyes on hers as he rubbed his chin, stubble about the length of Tate's. "You must sleep." He paused, a solemn expression returning. "One wish I might make is to touch upon you."

Mallory blinked a few times, unsure what he was saying, but instead of feeling uncomfortable, she felt . . . something else. "Do you mean . . ." She could feel herself blushing.

He smiled. "I say wrong." Then he chuckled, which

caused Mallory to smile. "Hold." He wrapped his arms around himself.

"Hug. You mean hug." She wrapped her arms around herself. "I'm sending you a hug."

"I send you blessings, my dear Mallory." Then he kissed the tips of his fingers and pressed them against the computer screen.

Mallory did the same. She watched his face fade from the screen. But she knew that she would be "seeing" Abdul again.

CHAPTER SEVEN

Tate woke up the next morning feeling like a total jerk. When he called Mallory, the call went to voice mail.

"Hey, baby, it's me." He paused, sighing. "I'm a jerk. No excuses. I was disappointed about the job, and I said some stupid stuff. I love you with every inch of my being. And I'm sorry. Call me."

He'd already called his mother and bowed out of their Sunday morning routine, unsure which he would miss most—communion with God or pancakes. He felt a pang of guilt, decided he could still talk to God, and he probably didn't deserve the pancakes just for having the thought. After he prayed he opened his laptop and tortured himself by reading the e-mail from Les again. Hoping for something lighter to alter his spirits, he opened Facebook and scrolled through his news feed. Mallory had posted something at three thirty this morning. No wonder she hadn't answered her phone. She was probably still sleeping. He read the post: WHOSE SOUL DO YOU TOUCH?

He read the three comments below. Her friend Ginger had written: HUH?? Not surprising. Ginger was sweet, but she didn't have a lot of layers. Vicky responded: THE ONE YOU LOVE, AND THE ONE WHO LOVES YOU. That seemed a little odd, since she'd only been divorced about a month. Maybe she'd already met someone.

The third response was from Soraya: SO ENJOYED DIN-NER LAST NIGHT. I THINK YOU TOUCH MANY SOULS, MY FRIEND. Then she'd put a smiley face.

Mallory was right about Soraya. The woman was classy, beautiful, and kind. She lit up any room she was in. And she seemed so genuine. He was regretful about the way he'd acted, although he'd saved the really mean stuff for the love of his life. He typed a comment: YOU TOUCH MY SOUL IN A WAY THAT NO ONE EVER HAS. I LOVE YOU.

A few seconds later his computer dinged with a new comment underneath his. From Soraya: TATE, IT WAS SO LOVELY TO MEET YOU.

He wrote back: SORAYA, IT WAS GREAT TO MEET YOU AND ISMAIL ALSO. PLEASE THANK ISMAIL AGAIN FOR DINNER.

He fed ET, gave him a quick scratch between the ears, then squatted to the floor to do his push-ups. He'd only done a dozen or so when his cell phone rang. He was surprised to see on the caller ID that it was Chantal. Probably calling to cancel Verdell's lesson for tomorrow. And that was fine with Tate.

"Tate. Tate. Is that you?"

"Yeah. Chantal? Is everything okay?" Tate stood up, walked to the couch, and sat down next to the cat.

"No, it's not. I'm sorry to bother you, but I didn't know who else to call. Can you keep Verdell if I bring him over there?"

"Uh . . ." Tate lifted his eyebrows. "What's wrong?" He'd been teaching—or babysitting—Verdell for the past six months, but it wasn't like Tate was a friend of the family or anything. Verdell was hard enough to deal with for an hour a week.

"I have a bit of an emergency, and my friend Sammy is nowhere to be found. I could probably leave him home alone. I mean, I guess he's old enough to stay by himself, but . . ."

Tate didn't know much about kids—outside of trying to teach them—but he was pretty sure ten was too young to be home alone. He didn't have anything going on today anyway. "Sure. Bring him over." After he hung up, he started thinking about a late breakfast. Surely Verdell ate pancakes. Should he whip out the box of pancake mix or take Verdell to IHOP?

He decided to scramble some eggs instead. He wasn't feeling worthy of pancakes this morning. He'd been mean to Mallory, and he'd skipped church. *But a guy's gotta eat.* He turned off the burner when the doorbell rang.

Verdell stood on the front step—with a red suitcase at his side? Chantal waved as she backed out of Tate's driveway.

MALLORY ROLLED OVER AND LOOKED AT THE CLOCK, startled that she'd slept until eleven. She reached for her cell phone, listened to Tate's message, then slowly crawled out of bed. She showered and dressed before she called him back.

"I'm sorry," he answered.

Mallory's head was still spinning with recollections of her conversations with Abdul until the early hours of the morning. And soon she was expected at Sunday dinner. Best to just get things fixed with Tate and move on. "Apology accepted."

"I was just upset about the job, but you're right . . . we have a lot to be thankful for. And I do feel bad for your friend's daughter. I'll start including her in my prayers. God is still in the miracle business, so He can heal her if it's His will."

Tate said that a lot—that God is still in the miracle business. Mallory wasn't so sure about that.

"I've got to go to my parents' house shortly. Sure you don't want to come?" She knew he wouldn't, but she asked every now and then just the same.

"I can't. You're not going to believe what happened."

Mallory poured herself some much-needed coffee as she yawned. "What? What happened? And why are you whispering?"

"I'm in my bedroom. Verdell's aunt called and asked if I could watch him for a while, which was kind of weird, but I said okay, thinking it would be for a couple of hours this afternoon." He paused. "But get this . . . the kid shows up with a suitcase!"

Mallory stopped pouring cream in her coffee. "What? How long are you supposed to keep him?"

"I don't know. Chantal's not answering her phone. I

asked Verdell how long he was planning to stay, and do you know what he said?"

Mallory waited.

"He said, 'You know she isn't coming back, right?'"

"What?" Mallory pulled out a chair at the kitchen table and sat down. "What does that mean?"

"I have no idea. What do I do if she doesn't show up by tomorrow? Do I call someone? Like CPS or something?"

"Did he say anything else?"

"Oh yeah . . . he said Chantal is heading to Oklahoma!"

Mallory could hear the panic in Tate's voice. "Wow. I don't know what you should do. Should I come over later?"

"That would be great. Maybe you'll have more luck talking to Verdell. I'm telling you, there is something wrong with that kid."

"I hope he can't hear you. And of course there is something wrong with him. His parents both died recently. That would mess anyone up, much less a ten-year-old."

"He can't hear me. I'm in my room with the door closed. But I'm glad you're coming. And I really am sorry about last night. Soraya and Ismail are great. They really are."

Mallory smiled. "It's okay, Tater Tot. I'll be there as soon as I can get away."

After they hung up, Mallory checked her e-mail, then looked at the posts underneath her Facebook comment. "I love you too, Tate," she said as she closed her laptop.

She showed up at her parents' house in jeans, flip-flops, and a pink T-shirt. She'd left with her hair wet, which felt good in the August heat.

Her parents and Vicky were already seated at the dining room table. To her disappointment, Haley and Braiden weren't there. School was starting the next day, and Nelson had taken the kids to Jumpstreet at Katy Mills Mall for a final summer fling.

Her father politely inquired about Tate—standard protocol for Sunday dinners. They'd given up asking why he didn't come. It was an uneventful meal, and Mallory was glad for that. She made her exit as soon as she could, then hurried to Tate's house.

Tate opened the door with a look of relief and motioned her into the living room, where Verdell was watching TV, and made the introductions.

"Hi, Verdell." Mallory walked to the couch, picked up ET, and gave the cat a scratch behind the ears. "And hello to you too, ET." She set the cat on the floor and sat down. "How are you?"

"Okay," the boy replied, not taking his eyes from the television screen. The cat rubbed up against him, then jumped into his lap. "Why is the cat's name ET?" He ran his hand the length of ET's back.

"Tate climbed a tree to rescue him," Mallory said. "Which was a pretty big deal for a guy afraid of heights! But ET turned out to be a bit different from other cats. He won't eat anything but dog food—brown dog food. I told Tate that his cat must be an alien, a cat from another planet. And the name ET stuck."

Verdell didn't respond, and Mallory realized that he might not have ever seen the movie. "You know, ET for extraterrestrial? ET was an alien in a fun movie." She paused. "So, um . . . how long will you be staying with Tate? Is your aunt going on a vacation?"

"I guess. She's going to Oklahoma." Verdell kept his eyes straight ahead.

Mallory glanced at Tate, who was looking a little pale.

"Okay. So is she planning on leaving you here for a long time?"

Verdell shrugged. "Forever, I guess."

There was a brief silence.

"I have a letter in my suitcase for you." Verdell looked at Tate.

"And you're just now telling me?" Tate stood up. He folded his arms across his chest and spoke extra calmly and slowly. "Verdell . . . can you get me the letter, please?"

Verdell lifted himself off of the couch and walked to his suitcase. He dug around, then pulled out a sealed envelope and handed it to Tate.

Mallory walked to where Tate was standing, and together they read the letter silently.

Dear Tate,

By the time you get this, I'll be on my way to Oklahoma. I know that you'll probably call the authorities, but I'm not really abandoning Verdell, as I've never had official custody of him anyway. I just started keeping him after his parents died since there was no will or directive about him, and I'm his only relative. He didn't have anywhere else to go.

I asked Verdell if he could live with anyone in the

world, who he would pick, and he chose you. I'm not sure why. Maybe you know? I think it is partly because you play the piano, which is something Verdell used to enjoy before his parents were killed. But I've also watched you with Verdell over the past six months. He's a handful, but you've never been too harsh with him.

I was afraid if I asked you, you would say no. It's a cowardly thing to do, I know. I'm going to be with the only man I've ever really loved—my ex-husband. And Verdell just isn't part of that package. His future will most likely depend on what you tell others, the school, etc. He could grow up in foster care, and the child has been through a lot.

You will have to make a decision as to what to do about Verdell. Please take care of him. He really is a good boy. I will miss him. And don't give up on his piano lessons.

Chantal

Mallory looked at Tate, who just shook his head. She looked at Verdell. ET was still curled up in his lap, and the boy was stroking the cat's back, his eyes glued to a cartoon on the television.

"Hey, Verdell. We'll be back, okay?" Tate latched onto Mallory's arm, and they crossed the living room to the front door.

"Tate?"

They both stopped and turned around when Verdell spoke. "Yeah, Verdell. What is it?"

Verdell eased the cat off his lap and stood up. He blinked his eyes a few times. "Are you going to give me away too?"

Mallory bit her lip, hoping Tate would come up with the right words. But he didn't move or speak, so Mallory moved toward Verdell, and once she was right in front of him, she said, "No one is going to give you away." She touched him on the top of his head. "And there's nothing for you to worry about, okay?"

Then she walked back to Tate, and they went outside.

"Why did you tell him that? We can't promise him something like that. What a mess." Tate threw his hands in the air. "What is wrong with that woman? She can't just drop him off like this because she is going to go be with her ex-husband. That's just nuts."

"Tate, no matter what happens, or how you decide to handle this, we don't want Verdell feeling like he's been given away. That's just a bad way to put it." Mallory paused. "Wow. What *are* you going to do, though?"

"I have no idea."

Chapter Eight

It was harder every day for Ismail to face Mallory. He'd heard from Abdul that he and Mallory were Skyping in the evenings. His cousin was a handsome man, and from what Ismail remembered, a charmer as well. All this deception was keeping Ismail awake at night. But Shahid Fahim was an evil man, and Ismail wasn't sure how far his father would go to get what he wanted.

"Hey, are you okay?" Mallory asked as she walked by his office.

He motioned for her to come in. Ismail had observed a kindness about Mallory that one just didn't find in everyone. Soraya had it too. Probably why they were becoming such good friends. And another reason why Ismail felt like a bottom dweller. If Mallory did end up going to help Majida, Ismail would pay for her trip, missed wages, and any other expenses. A small price to pay. He wondered what else he could do for her—anything to ease the guilt.

"I'm just worried about my niece, Majida. Abdul is doing everything he can, and I've offered to help him financially, but there just isn't much hope for his beautiful daughter unless we can find a way to get her here."

Mallory sat down in one of the chairs facing Ismail's desk. "I know. I asked Abdul if Lahore or Dubai was an option, but he didn't think so. He said they don't have health insurance."

"Abdul is checking on several things. He and Fozia are committed to do whatever it takes to save their child." Ismail paused. "Even though they are divorced."

"I think it's wonderful the way they get along so well." Mallory folded her hands in her lap. "You know, we've talked a lot over the past couple weeks . . . Abdul and I. We just kind of hit it off. I know he's desperate to help his daughter."

Ismail wondered what Tate thought about her friendship with Abdul. Or if he even knew.

"Yes. Abdul told me that he treasures your friendship very much. He was hoping to come here for our wedding, but without a sponsor it is impossible. So we will see him in Lahore for the second wedding. And hopefully Majida will still be with us." He bowed his head. "Praise be to Allah—peace be upon him."

"There has to be a solution. We just haven't thought of it yet." Mallory leaned back in the chair.

Oh, you'd be surprised what everyone has thought of.

Ismail had hoped that Mallory would have done the research by now and figured out the solution on her own—so that he wouldn't have to keep piling one lie on top of another. But apparently he needed to lure her closer to the edge before he pushed her over. He took a deep breath.

"I have reached out to several friends—single women—who might be interested in going to Peshawar. I've offered them a hefty sum of money to do so."

Lies, lies. Ismail didn't know anyone stupid enough to go to that part of Pakistan, not even for money.

"How would that help Majida?"

"If Abdul was to marry an American woman, it would expedite sponsorship . . . in part because he would be married, but more so because of Majida's health needs."

This was all true, to the best of Ismail's knowledge, but Peshawar wasn't a safe place for anyone to travel. Someone like Mallory, with her blond hair and fair skin, would be easy prey. And there were plenty of people who would kill a person just because of that person's skin color or nationality. But Abdul had assured Ismail that he would keep Mallory safe. He had to trust his cousin about that, because if anything happened to Mallory, Abdul's family would be dishonored.

"I didn't realize that," she said. "Are you having any luck finding someone?"

Ismail shook his head. "Several women would like to, but there are different things preventing them from doing so. One of them has a child, and another one can't get off work. I thought someone had come through, but she is having her own health problems."

Ismail glanced at his watch. No patients for another twenty minutes. *Plenty of time to drive in the stake.*

"In Islam, if you do something so unselfishly, like this kind act would be, then you are guaranteed a place in paradise. So I am still looking for someone to help Majida."

Mallory tapped her fingers on the side of the chair. "Hmm . . ."

Ismail waited, then decided to pull a card from Mallory's Good Book. "As your Scripture says, greater love has no one than this: to lay down one's life for one's friends." He silently prayed that Allah wouldn't strike him down for what he was doing. "Not totally relevant, since I'm not asking anyone to give their life." He smiled.

Mallory nodded and looked thoughtful. But then she stood up. "I really hope you can find someone. Majida is so young. I'm sure Abdul will keep me posted. Thanks for telling me all this."

Ismail gave a taut bow of his head. "You're welcome." Then he glanced up, as though he'd just thought of something important. "Oh, and Mallory . . . I really hate to ask you to keep secrets from your friend, but please don't say anything to Soraya about this. I love my Soraya, but she has the wrong impression of Peshawar. She's never even been there, but she believes everything she sees on the news. The media misrepresents the place of my birth, never showing the true beauty and peacefulness to be found there." He shook his head. "But just the same, I would like to keep peace with Soraya, and she would be upset with me if she thought I was trying to find a wife-for-hire for Abdul."

And she would absolutely kill me if she thought I was putting the idea into your head.

MALLORY PUT THE PAN OF LASAGNA INTO THE OVEN and set the timer. Tate wouldn't be at her house for at least an hour. She went back to the couch and resumed her research on Peshawar.

Ismail couldn't have been any more transparent. Her boss knew she wanted to save a life, and he was clearly planting the idea in her head. She couldn't blame him for wanting to help his niece. Abdul had told her the same thing as Ismail— that the media only showed the ugly parts of the country, that where he lived was very safe and beautiful. But as she scoured the Internet, she found photos to validate both the beauty of Pakistan and the fact that it was a war-torn country.

She'd been thinking about her cousin Kelsey all day. Would bringing Majida to the United States guarantee Mallory a place in heaven—or paradise, as Ismail called it? *Greater love has no one than this: to lay down one's life for one's friends.* She knew it was in the Bible, but she couldn't recall who said it. She wished her parents had raised her and Vicky in the church. She should have at least been properly introduced to God when she was young. At the very least, would helping Majida ease her guilt over not being able to save Kelsey?

She tried to picture the look on Tate's face if she told him that she was going to Pakistan to marry Abdul and hopefully save his daughter's life. He would have a fit, even if it was a marriage in name only. Then she thought about her mother and father and Vicky; it was a toss-up as to which of them would be most upset. But then, somewhere in the midst of all the negativity, she pictured the look on Abdul's face if she told him she was considering a way to help him and Majida. A very different vision.

Surprisingly, there were quite a few travel websites showcasing things to do in Peshawar. But all of them had a travel warning at the top directing the user to the US Department of State, which recommended that all nonessential travel to the country be avoided.

Mallory recalled her trip to Mexico with three girlfriends five years ago. Her parents had begged her not to go. But one passport and eight hundred dollars later, she'd had a wonderful time—despite the warnings about drug lords, kidnappings, and the dangers for Americans.

Her next search was to determine the documents she would need. She already had a passport, but tourists also needed a visa. Just then her cell phone vibrated. Soraya. Mallory answered and told her friend what she was considering.

"Mallory, did Abdul put this idea in your head?"

"No." *Your fiancé did.*

"Well, good. I would be very angry if he was trying to lure you over there. You must *never* go to Peshawar. Do you understand me?" Soraya's voice didn't have the cheerfulness that Mallory loved. "Just tell me you will not consider this."

"I'm not saying I would go. I was just doing the research." But she was surprised at Soraya's strong reaction. "But, Soraya, it can't be that dangerous—you're going there for your wedding."

"I am going to Lahore, not Peshawar. That's a tribal area, Mallory. It would never be safe for you to go there."

"What if this is my chance to make a difference?"

"This is not the opportunity you're looking for. Promise me you'll give the matter no more thought."

"But what an adventure it would be," Mallory said softly.

Soraya rattled off something in another language, then switched back to English. "*Mis*adventure would be more accurate. You just banish any thoughts about such a foolish idea."

"Wow. You really don't like Peshawar, do you?"

"It's just not safe, Mallory. You have lived here all your life. You can't even imagine what it's like there. Women are treated badly. Do you even know what sharia law is?"

Soraya continued before Mallory had a chance to tell her she'd read about it.

"The interpretations vary depending on where you live. It's meant to be the moral code and religious law of Islam, but translations are sketchy at best. Anyway, you're just going to have to trust me on this."

"How long were you in Peshawar?"

"I grew up in Lahore. It's an eight-hour drive between the two cities."

Mallory thought about her conversation with Ismail. "I know. I was just wondering how much time you've actually spent in Peshawar."

Soraya didn't try to hide her frustration. "I have never been there, but Mallory—"

"How can you say all this if you've never been there? You can pick up a Houston newspaper and find stories of people being murdered on the streets. What's the difference? It's a chance we take every time we walk out of our house."

"My parents have been there. I have friends who have been there. I wish you would just trust me on this." Soraya paused briefly, then changed the subject. "Anyway, the reason I am calling is to let you know I have collected the piano music I'd like Tate to play at the reception. I'll send it with Ismail tomorrow. But I'm totally open to Tate's suggestions as well."

"That sounds great."

When Tate arrived, Mallory was still researching online. She wasn't sure she was ready to tell Tate what she was considering, though. She was pretty sure it would blow up in a fight.

"GREAT LASAGNA," TATE SAID AS THEY WALKED TO THE living room. He was thankful his mother had agreed to stay with Verdell and give Tate a free Friday night. Mallory had been distant ever since their fight after the dinner with Ismail and Soraya, and he was looking forward to some alone time with her.

They sat down on the couch, and as he was pulling her into his arms, Tate noticed a book on the coffee table. "Whoa, what's that? What are you doing with a copy of the Quran?"

She stayed nuzzled up against him, her head against his chest. "I'm reading it."

Tate eased her away until their eyes met. "Why?"

"Why not?" She shrugged.

Tate thought about all the times he'd asked her if maybe she'd like to read the Bible. His mother had even invited her to a women's Bible study last year, and Mallory had made up an excuse not to go. "I guess I'm wondering why you don't want to read the Bible but you're reading the Quran."

She raised her eyebrows. "I already know what the Bible says."

"How could you know? You haven't read it."

She let out a small grunt. "Tate, I know about Christianity. I believe in God. I've learned things from you. And yes, I do know some of the Bible."

Tate rubbed the stubble on his chin. "I would think that you'd want to read the Bible before the Quran, that's all."

"You know I like to learn new things. Ismail and Soraya are both Muslim, and I thought it might be nice to learn more about their beliefs. I really don't know anything at all about Islam."

Tate nodded, wanting that to make sense. Maybe if Mallory were stronger in her Christian faith he wouldn't have an issue with it. "I just think you should understand what it means to be a Christian before you go the opposite direction and read a book that doesn't acknowledge the Trinity."

"Well, they worship the same God we do, and Islam is a peaceful religion."

Tate got up and paced about her living room, then looked down at his girlfriend. An outsider, looking at those big, innocent, doe eyes of hers, might think Mallory wasn't the sharpest tool in the shed, but Tate knew she was intelligent. "They don't believe Jesus is the Son of God."

"But they do believe in Jesus. I haven't actually read very much of the Quran yet. It was easier to look up things on the Internet and get a summary. But I intend to read it." She folded her arms across her chest.

Tate came back and sat down with her again. "That's fine, Mallory. I just don't understand why you don't show that much interest in the Bible."

"If it'll make you happy, Tate, I'll read the Bible too."

Tate forced a smile. "Maybe read that *before* you read a book that doesn't go along with our beliefs."

Mallory pressed her lips firmly together. "How does either one of us know which book is the truth?"

Mallory was always hungry for knowledge, and she'd question just about anything. But this was a subject he wasn't going to debate with her. "Never mind."

They'd had this argument before. Not about Islam, but about organized religion in general. They were just starting to get back on solid ground, and Tate didn't want to take a step backward.

"What do you mean, never mind?"

"Don't pick a fight, Mallory. We're just in two different places when it comes to our faith."

"I'm not trying to pick a fight, Tate. I'm just asking. How does anyone know which religion is really the right one? What if I had been born in Pakistan? I'd probably believe Muhammad to be the greatest of prophets, and I wouldn't believe Jesus was the Son of God. I'd practice the five pillars of Islam, partake in Ramadan, and—"

"Wow, Mallory . . . how much did you read?"

She pointed a finger at him. "It's because you're Catholic. You think everyone should be Catholic."

This was quickly going from a friendly debate to a fight. "That's not true, and you know it."

She crossed her arms across her chest again. "Do you believe that a person must believe in Jesus as their Savior to go to heaven?"

They'd had this discussion before too. "Yes. I do."

"Well, lots of Muslims believe that Christians will go to what they call paradise. But some are like you and believe that only those practicing Islam will go."

"You learned all this by scanning the Internet and flipping through the Quran?"

Mallory shrugged. "I would have hidden the book if I'd known it was going to blow into this big a deal."

"Does this have anything to do with your new friend? What's his name, Abdul? Exactly how much do you talk to this guy?"

Tate wasn't usually jealous, and he didn't care if she had a male friend, but if this man was trying to sway her to Islam, he was going to have a huge problem with that.

"It doesn't have anything to do with Abdul. He doesn't push me about religion the way you do."

"I don't push you," Tate said softly. Disappointment washed over him. "I should probably go home, since my mom is there watching Verdell."

Mallory stood. "It's just a friendly debate, Tate. But if I don't agree with you, then you get mad. I should be able to search for what works for me. I just don't feel like I have any direction."

Tate stood too. "If you need direction, Mallory, turn to God. God the Father, the Son, and the Holy Spirit. *Our* God."

"Muslims pray to the same God we do," she said.

"Uh . . . no. I don't pray to Allah. And when you're doing your comparisons between Christianity and Islam, be sure to research the parts about sharia law, jihad, and how Muhammad told Muslims to wage war on other religions to bring them under submission to Islam." He pointed his finger at her. "I've done my homework. And I don't like what I learned."

"Everything is black-and-white with you, Tate. And there are a lot of gray areas where Christians are concerned. There are good and bad people in every religion."

Tate wasn't sure what to say. He understood that Mallory's free spirit had to fly, but he hoped that when she landed, the two of them would be in the same place.

AS THE DOOR CLOSED BEHIND TATE, MALLORY FOUGHT the urge to cry. Tate was the best man she'd ever known, but when it came to religion, he walked a straight line. She heard a Skype call coming in, and she knew it could only be Abdul.

"Why is my dear Mallory sad?" he asked when she answered the call. The man had a full plate, yet he still showed genuine concern about her well-being.

"Rough evening with Tate." She filled him in on the details. At first it felt like betrayal to share something so personal about her relationship with Tate, but Abdul was so kind and understanding, so complimentary, so sympathetic.

"It saddens my heart to hear this," he said. "Islam not understood by Christian Americans. We have many Christians here. My children are schooled at the St. Mary's School. Is run by the Roman Catholic Church."

Mallory widened her eyes. "Wow. Really?" She couldn't wait to tell Tate that Abdul's children went to a Catholic school. That was bound to blow some of his theories out of the water.

The screen went blank—probably another blackout, something that happened frequently when she was Skyping with Abdul.

Soon he called back and locked eyes with her from across the world.

"I am sorry. Bad is our electricity." He gave her a gentle smile. "You will find your way, my dear Mallory, and you will see Allah in your heart, feel him in your soul. In prayer I will keep your Tate, as you have Majida. Prayers will be for under-standing, for peace." He paused. "Will you pray with me, my dear Mallory?"

"Of course." She lowered her head and closed her eyes, waiting.

"Can you say aloud? I understand more better than I speak English."

Mallory nodded, then lowered her head. She'd never led a prayer out loud, and she really wasn't clear about how to talk to God, silently or otherwise.

"Dear God . . ." She hesitated, trying to recall what Regina usually prayed for. "Please wrap Your loving arms around Abdul, Majida, and their entire family. We ask . . . we ask that You heal her." Pausing, she actually prayed silently for God to give her the words. "You are an all-loving God who can

make Majida well. Please, dear Lord, heal Abdul's daughter."
She stopped, thinking about how Regina always ended prayer
by saying, "In Jesus' name we pray." Instead, she just said,
"Amen," and opened her eyes.

Abdul nodded. "*Alhamdulillah*," he said, then smiled slightly.
"That means that all praises are due to God."

Mallory tried to smile. She wondered what Tate would
think about her praying with Abdul.

"We both worship the same God, my dear Mallory. Your
Tate will come to know this. It is of no harm for us to pray
together. And *insha Allah*—God willing—he will make my
Majida new again."

She liked that about Abdul, how he seemed to know just
what she was thinking sometimes. But if God could do anything, why did He allow sick children in the world? "Is there
anything I can do, Abdul? I mean, aside from praying for
Majida."

"Yes." He smiled again. "Give me a deception."

Mallory bit her bottom lip. "Deception?"

"Yes. So no thoughts about Majida come to my mind."

"Do you mean *distraction*? You want me to talk about
something else to get your mind off of this?"

Abdul nodded, and they talked for the next three hours.
About all kinds of things. Relationships, children, spiritual
beliefs, even food. Mallory found Abdul to be a wonderful
distraction as well.

And by the end of the phone call, she knew that God was
giving her a second chance to make a difference.

CHAPTER NINE

By noon the next day, Tate had left three messages for Mallory with no return call. By the third one, he'd apologized, something he should have done in the first place. He'd yelled at Verdell for no real reason. Tate knew he needed to call someone about the kid, but every time he picked up the phone to call Child Protective Services, he just couldn't go through with it. He'd also been leaving messages for Chantal.

He sat down at his kitchen table and called Mallory again. This time she answered.

"I really am sorry," he said. "I'm not sure how things blew up the way they did."

"I'm not either. But I'm really bothered by the way you feel about Muslims."

He rested his forehead in his hand. "You know I'm not

prejudiced. You know that about me, baby. It's just that . . . those people scare me. I'm not like your parents, but—"

"Last night you acted just like my parents."

Tate tried to choose his words carefully. "Maybe it seemed that way, but I don't hate Muslims, Mallory. And I get the fact that you need to be on your own faith journey. My mom calls herself a 'daughter of the promise.' It's when a woman—or anyone really—goes on a spiritual journey to find new meaning to the words *faith, hope,* and *love.* Maybe I need to give you the space to travel your own journey."

Mallory was quiet for a few seconds. "I'm glad you feel that way, because I think we need some space too. Maybe take a break for a while."

Tate's heart pounded in his chest. "I meant space for you to find your own spiritual path. Not put space between *us,* as in our relationship. I don't want a break."

"I love you with all my heart, Tate. But I don't feel like we've been treating each other very well lately. All sorts of things are fueling our arguments."

"Baby, no. I love you. We're not breaking up, are we?"

"Not breaking up—just taking a break. I've already talked to Ismail about taking a little time from work. A sabbatical, I guess you could say."

"A sabbatical? Mallory, you've only been working there a few months."

"I know—call it vacation then. This doesn't mean I don't love you and want to spend the rest of my life with you, but I think I need to take a little time for myself."

"How much time?" Tate put a hand on his chest, wondering

if this was what it felt like to have a heart attack, or if a broken heart could really cause this much physical pain.

"I don't know."

His eyes teared up. "I love you with all my heart, Mallory."

"I know, Tate. And I love you too."

He wished she'd call him Tater Tot. "I'll give you some space, Mallory. But please don't stay away long."

A FEW HOURS AFTER HER PHONE CALL WITH TATE, Mallory called Abdul via Skype. She knew it was late at night in Peshawar, but she had to talk to him.

"My dear Mallory," he said as he rubbed his eyes. "Are you in harm? Hurt?"

"I'm sorry I woke you. But I have something to tell you, something very important."

He blinked his eyes a few times. "If harm has come to you, I . . . I . . ." He shook his head. "Tell me you are well."

She smiled. "Yes, I am well. And I have made a decision. There is a way that we can get Majida here to the United States for treatment."

He brought a hand to his chest. "You speak of miracles."

"Abdul, I've told you how I want to save a life, to make a difference. And I've figured out a way to do that."

"Is this teasing?" He blinked his eyes again.

"No, my friend." She touched the computer screen with two fingers. "I'm not teasing. If I come to Peshawar and marry you, it will speed up the sponsorship process. At least that's what Ismail believes. Because of Majida's leukemia, I should be able to bring the two of you back to the United States much quicker. It might not happen on my first trip there, but we could get the ball rolling." She bit her lip, then said, "Of course the marriage would be in name only. You know how much I love Tate, and I still intend to marry him. I'd get a divorce after Majida is well."

Abdul lowered his head as his shoulders rose and fell.

"Oh, sweet Abdul. Don't cry."

He looked up at her, and a tear rolled down his cheek. "Why would you do this for my family?"

She smiled. "Because I can."

His bottom lip trembled. "Just when there is fear of no hope, Allah sends an angel, a beautiful woman with pure heart of love. But are you not afraid to be here, with all the bad words Soraya and your Tate tell you of Pakistan?"

Mallory tipped her head to one side and smiled. "Abdul, are you going to let anything happen to me?"

He scowled. "There will never come harm to you. I would die before harm touches you."

"I know." She knew this gentle man would keep her safe. "I know that there are dangers involved in this decision, but the outcome for Majida outweighs them. But I am going to need a letter of invitation from you to apply for a visa. Is this something you can do for me? Can you e-mail it to me?"

He dabbed at his eyes with a white handkerchief. "I will do anything for you. I will be owed to you for rest of my life."

She shook her head. "No, Abdul. You won't owe me. This is a gift."

"There could be hope for Majida?"

"Yes. Ismail spent time with a specialist familiar with her condition, and it is serious, so we need to move quickly. I'm going to come as soon as I can make arrangements."

"I—I will send you money on the wire."

Mallory shook her head. "I don't need money, Abdul. I have a trust fund—a big savings account my parents set up. You save your money for traveling here."

He gazed at her. "You are true angel."

"No." A warm feeling spread over her. "Just someone helping a friend." *And fulfilling a promise I made long ago.*

ON MONDAY MALLORY ASKED VICKY TO MEET HER FOR lunch.

"I have some errands to run near your office," Vicky said, "so I'll pick you up."

Mallory knew she could trust her sister to keep a secret from their parents. They'd kept plenty for each other over the years, even though they weren't particularly close. And since Vicky didn't have any special attachment to Tate, it wouldn't be a problem for her to keep a secret from him either.

"Can I try one more time to talk you out of this?" asked Vicky toward the end of the meal.

Mallory shook her head, and after she paid the bill, they headed to Vicky's car. She put on her sunglasses and gave her sister a final reminder. "And remember, you've promised not to tell Mom and Dad or Tate until I'm on the plane."

Vicky unlocked the car, and the two sisters got in. "How

much of this is because you're upset with Tate? And how much is because you're attracted to Abdul?"

"This is about Majida. She's only sixteen years old. Same age Kelsey was."

"Mom and Dad are going to absolutely flip out."

"I know."

"What have Ismail and his fiancée said?"

"Soraya. Her name is Soraya." Mallory swallowed hard as she recalled her conversation with Soraya the day before. "She tried to talk me out of it. She thinks it's a huge mistake. Ismail has a vested interest since Majida is his niece, so he is paying me while I'm off. He even offered to pay for my plane ticket, but I told him I would do that. Ismail thinks it's a very unselfish act of kindness to save his niece."

Vicky pulled out into traffic and didn't respond.

"He is actually encouraging," Mallory continued. "He said the same thing that Abdul said, that the news only shows the ugly stuff over there. Abdul is planning to take me to some amazing places. I don't think it's nearly as dangerous as people here think. And I know that Abdul will keep me safe."

"I certainly hope you're right."

Me too.

TATE PICKED VERDELL UP FROM SCHOOL. HE TRIED TO talk to the kid about his day, but Verdell was about as interested in the conversation as he was in the piano. Tate offered him some Oreos when they got home, but Verdell didn't want any.

The boy picked up ET and sat down on the couch with

the cat in his lap. "Why don't you just call someone to come get me?" he asked. "I know that's what you want to do."

Tate couldn't deny that, but he walked to the couch and sat down beside Verdell. "Why did you tell your aunt you wanted to come stay here in the first place?"

Verdell shrugged, enough for ET to get uncomfortable and jump down.

"Dude, I know nothing about being a parent or taking care of a kid. I'm just a piano player trying to make a living doing what I love." Tate's heart was still so heavy. He was afraid to say too much or he might burst into tears.

"Is Mallory coming over?"

Tate shook his head. "Not tonight."

"Why aren't you and her married?"

Tate propped his elbows on his knees, then covered his face with his hands. "That's the million-dollar question." He looked up and forced a smile.

Verdell didn't say anything, and Tate handed him the remote control. "I don't have any students this afternoon, so knock yourself out. Or do you want to just talk?"

Verdell glanced at his backpack. "My mom used to help me with my homework. Aunt Chantal never did. But it was okay because I knew how to do the work. I think it made Mom feel good to help me."

This was the first time Verdell had mentioned his parents.

"It sounds like you and your mom were pretty close." Tate paused. "I'm close to my mom too."

"Your mom is nice."

"She's great."

Verdell lowered his head. "I don't think I'll ever be happy again."

Tate could feel the knot swelling in his throat as he swallowed back tears, wondering the same thing about himself.

ISMAIL FROWNED WHEN SORAYA SAID SHE WAS LEAVING to go to Mallory's. "What's in the bag?" he asked, nodding to the green tote she was carrying.

"*Salwar*, a *kameez*, and a *dupatta*. They're very old, from when I was young in Lahore. I'm taking them to Mallory to wear on her trip. Otherwise she'll really stand out. I still cannot believe she is doing this." Soraya squinted at him. "I hope you've been trying to discourage her from going. I know her heart is in the right place, but this is a terrible idea. I've actually been praying that her visa will be denied." She pointed a finger at him. "You should have denied her the time off from work."

"Mallory is a grown woman. I can't control what she does. And she's been here half a year, so she's earned a week off." Ismail had been having heart palpitations, and he'd been praying it was just nerves. It was exhausting to try to make Peshawar sound like anything other than what it was—a miserable place. Yet he'd been feeding Mallory a hefty dose of lies so she'd seal the deal. During the day it seemed justifiable. But at night—when he had to leave work and face Soraya—he felt like a louse.

"She's planning to stay *two* weeks. You could have denied her the second." Soraya huffed as she passed by him on the couch. "You of all people know what life in Peshawar is like."

"And you do not, my beloved. You've never been there."

"I know enough. And Mallory has such a fair complexion and blond hair." She raised the bag. "At least she can cover up her body. I don't know what she'll do about those big blue eyes. I'll remind her to wear sunglasses."

If anything happened to Mallory, Ismail wasn't sure he would be able to forgive himself. He had to trust that Abdul would keep her safe. He planned to pray constantly for her. As much as he wanted his niece to have proper medical care, he still couldn't believe the extremes his father had resorted to in an effort to get Abdul a wife.

"What does Tate say about her going?" He cringed, thinking about the poor guy.

"He doesn't know. And she made me promise not to tell him. They've been having some problems. Mallory said they are just taking a break. But Tate is going to be very upset when he finds out."

Ismail sat taller. "Abdul is a good man. He will protect her at all costs." Ismail silently prayed for Allah to forgive his lies.

"You don't know if he is a good man or not. You haven't known him since you were boys." Soraya shook her head as she moved toward the door.

"Are you coming back tonight?"

"I don't know." Soraya blew him a kiss, but Ismail suspected she wasn't.

MALLORY LET SORAYA IN. "PLEASE TELL ME YOU'RE not going to try to talk me out of going again."

"No. I brought you something." She handed Mallory the

bag she was carrying. "I found these things in the back of my closet. They're very old but better than nothing. You need to wear them for your travels."

Mallory pulled out the clothes. "Thank you. Abdul said he would have sent me some clothes, but since I'm planning to leave next week, there isn't time."

"What if you don't have your visa by then?"

"I paid to get it expedited, but if it doesn't get here in time, I'll just have to push back the flight." She motioned for Soraya to follow her to her bedroom. "I always pack days ahead of time. This is what I'm planning to take." She pointed to the four pairs of jeans she had laid out, several blouses, and some slacks.

"If I were you, I wouldn't wear any of that." Soraya paused. "Do you ever read the news? You are going to a third-world, predominantly Muslim country, filled with people who hate Americans. And all of this screams American. Wear what I gave you, and tell Abdul to have some clothes for you when you arrive."

Mallory went into the bathroom and tried on the clothes, then walked back into the bedroom. "Am I wearing this scarf thing correctly?"

"It's called a dupatta." Soraya stood up, made some adjustments to the scarf, then gently grabbed Mallory's shoulders and turned her toward the mirror. "Like that."

"This is super comfortable."

"Glad you like it." Soraya rolled her eyes. "So tell me. When is your return flight?"

"I'm only staying two weeks. I told Abdul that I would like to meet his family and we could talk about my helping

Abdul and Majida get here. If our getting married will expedite Majida's trip to the States, then that's what we'll do."

"Your handsome Tate is going to be very upset about this. I think he would forbid you to go."

"Well, Tate could not *forbid* me to go. He doesn't control me." Mallory was reminded of their differing backgrounds, no matter how American her friend was now. Although she'd never heard Ismail deny his fiancée anything she wanted. Mallory eased her way back into the bathroom, talking as she took off her traveling clothes. "But he would throw a fit. So I'm just going to go while we are taking this little break."

"Yet you are going to a country where that is the normal behavior, the men controlling the women."

"It's only a visit, Soraya. And Abdul is not going to let anything happen to me." Mallory came back into the bedroom. "Everything will be fine."

"I hope so." Soraya picked up the Quran on Mallory's nightstand. "Are you reading this?"

Mallory finished buttoning her shirt. "I've read a little." She thought about her fight with Tate.

"Why?"

Mallory shrugged. "Just curious, I guess. You and Ismail are Muslim, and Abdul. So I'm just reading up on Islam."

Soraya stared at her. "I don't believe you, Mallory. Why are you really reading it?"

Mallory stood taller, a bit taken aback. "What do you mean? I don't understand."

"I asked why you are *really* reading the Quran. I don't think it's just curiosity."

"Well . . ." She wasn't sure what Soraya was hoping she'd say.

"I'm just asking *why* you are curious. Think about it for a minute."

Mallory had thought about it, in exactly the same sense that she feared Soraya was getting at. How did her friend know what was going on in Mallory's mind?

"It's the oneness with God." She lowered her head, knowing Tate would be destroyed if he knew that Mallory was questioning Jesus' role in her life. "Sometimes I have trouble believing that the Father, the Son, and the Holy Spirit are all the same." She bit her bottom lip. "Soraya, I haven't stopped believing that Jesus is the Son of God. I just . . ."

"You don't have to explain to me, Mallory." Soraya smiled. "I don't believe that Jesus, peace be upon him, is the Son of God, but he is one of our most holy prophets. And I don't expect you to believe as I do." She shrugged. "But be honest with yourself."

Mallory felt like she might cry. "I guess I just get confused sometimes. I didn't really grow up in church. My family just proclaimed themselves to be Christian, so I was automatically expected to do the same, even though I didn't really understand why. Tate is Catholic, so our opinions about religion cause friction sometimes."

They were quiet for a moment.

"Well, I will be anxiously awaiting your safe arrival home, and I will want to hear all about your trip."

"I'm sure it will be a grand adventure. Something I'll remember for the rest of my life."

CHAPTER TEN

It had been nearly two weeks since Tate talked to Mallory. He was trying to give her the space she wanted, but he missed her. He and Verdell had settled into a routine surprisingly well, and Verdell even smiled now and again. It was a messed-up situation, but Tate still wasn't ready to send the child packing, off with strangers. Chantal had finally returned his phone call, and she admitted that what she'd done was crazy. But in the end Tate had agreed to keep Verdell for a while. Tonight Tate's mother was coming over, and she was bringing her famous chicken enchiladas. The only thing missing was Mallory.

"Hello, Verdell." Mom handed Tate the casserole dish. "It sure is nice to see you again. We had fun playing cards last time, didn't we? Even though you beat me every time." Mom rolled her bottom lip under into a pout.

Verdell smiled. Such a small thing, but for Verdell it was huge. Mom could usually wrangle a smile out of anyone.

Tate breathed in the zesty aroma of the enchiladas. "These smell great, Mom."

They all walked into the kitchen. "They're so easy to make. I've given you the recipe before."

"I know. And I made them for Mallory once, but they just weren't the same." He pulled three plates from the shelf and put them on the table. "Verdell, you'll love these."

"They smell good." Verdell smiled again as he pulled out his chair and sat down.

Tate's cell phone buzzed on the counter. His mom pointed to it. "You tell whoever that is that we're eating."

But Tate picked up the phone. "I gotta get this. It's Mallory's sister. Vicky never calls."

"Tate?"

"Yeah. Is Mallory okay?"

"Well . . . I mean, yes. She's okay, but . . ."

"But what? Vicky, what's wrong?"

"Tate, she's okay. I think. I mean . . . oh man. She's going to kill me. I promised her that I wouldn't tell you until she was on the plane, but I just dropped her off at the airport and I'm worried sick."

"Airport?" Tate hurried into the living room. "Where's she going?"

"Pakistan."

Tate sat down on the couch before he fell down. "What? Are you kidding me?"

"No. She is going to meet her friend Abdul. He has a sick daughter, and Mallory thinks she might be able to help, and—"

"What time is her flight?" He was grabbing his keys and wallet from the coffee table as he spoke.

"In about an hour. I'm really worried. Our parents don't know either. I should have called earlier, but I wasn't sure what to do. She made me promise. But since you aren't too far from the airport, I thought you might be able to stop her. She's gonna kill me, but I'm just scared for her."

Tate pulled the phone from his face to holler for his mother, then asked Vicky, "What terminal? What airline?"

As his mother scurried into the room with Verdell close behind, Tate thanked Vicky and hung up. "Mom, can you stay with Verdell until I get back? Mallory is about to do something really stupid, and I have to get to her."

"Of course, honey. Go, go. Verdell and I will be fine. What's going on?"

Tate bit off a curse word he rarely used. "She's actually about to fly to Pakistan."

He ran out the door and peeled out of the driveway. Normally he could be at the airport in about twenty minutes, but that was without traffic. He hurried onto the beltway, thanking God that there wasn't a backup at the tollbooth.

He dialed her number, and of course it went straight to voice mail.

"Baby, don't do this. I love you with all my heart. We just need to talk. I was trying to give you the space you wanted." His voice cracked. "Mallory, please. What you're doing is dangerous. Please don't get on that plane. I'm on my way to the airport. Don't be mad at Vicky. I love you." He paused. "Don't get on that plane."

MALLORY LISTENED TO TATE'S VOICE MAIL, DETERMINED not to cry. She'd already been on the phone with Abdul earlier, and he and his family were excited for her arrival. She was sure this was the right thing to do. It would be the adventure of a lifetime. She was wearing the clothes she'd borrowed from Soraya, who had also called her today and tried to talk her out of going.

She'd halfway expected Vicky to do this, to tell Tate before she was off the ground and on her way. Vicky had insisted on parking instead of just using the drop-off lane. When they'd gotten inside the airport, her sister had tried again to change Mallory's mind and even started to cry. But with a final hug good-bye, Mallory told her that everything would be fine.

Then she turned off her phone. She didn't want anyone else trying to scare her out of this trip. She reminded herself why she was going, and she was trying not to panic because the security line was moving so slowly. She'd checked one large suitcase and was carrying her purse and laptop.

Relief washed over her after she cleared security, but not without being patted down first. She felt a little ridiculous in the clothes she'd borrowed from Soraya, but the pastel colors were pretty and the flat loafers she'd chosen would help with all the walking. The only thing bugging her was the head covering, a scarf that wrapped over her head and around her neck. Soraya had told her not to wear any makeup, but she didn't want to meet Abdul and his family without any, so she'd tucked blush, mascara, and a light pink lipstick into her purse.

After she gathered her purse and laptop, she sat down on a bench. She still had nearly an hour before they would start boarding the flight. Her original plan had been to eat before she got on the plane, then take some Benadryl to help with the pressure pain she sometimes got when she flew. Plus she hoped it would knock her out on this first leg of her journey. But she'd lost her appetite somewhere between the parking lot and security. She pulled her purse up on her shoulder and started walking. But then she heard her name called—loudly— from the other side of security. She couldn't believe it.

Two security guards were already on their way to Tate, but that didn't stop him from bellowing at her.

"Mallory, don't do this! Don't go!"

She turned and they locked eyes, and Mallory was tempted to run to him.

"Mallory, I love you!"

But by now there were three security guards at Tate's side, and he was busy talking to them, probably trying not to get arrested. People were whispering and pointing, but Tate yelled at her again, louder this time.

"Don't go, Mallory!"

She blinked her eyes a few times, and even though she knew he couldn't hear her, she whispered, "Bye, Tate" and forced herself to turn and head toward her gate. A sick feeling hung in her gut. It wasn't too late to forget this entire thing and run back to him. But she was determined to live out this experience—a leap of faith. She didn't turn around as she headed toward the gate, even though it was taking great effort to put one foot in front of the other.

TATE SHOOK LOOSE OF THE SECURITY PERSONNEL who had latched onto his arm.

"Sir, you need to quiet down. I'm assuming this is a domestic matter, but you can't be acting like a madman in the airport. I'm going to ask you to leave. Now."

There was no reason for him to stay. "I'm going." He headed toward the exit, praying the entire time that God would keep Mallory safe and bring her back and into his arms. He was incredibly angry, but fear was suffocating him. When he got to the car, he called her phone number again.

"It's not too late, baby. I know you're not on the plane yet. Google 'Pakistan.' Read the government warnings on travel there. I love you, baby, and I'm scared for you. Please don't do this."

He sat in his car for a while, hoping and praying she'd call him back, saying she'd changed her mind. What could have motivated her to do this? He knew all about her promise to Kelsey, of course, but a much more disturbing thought had surfaced in his mind. *Had she fallen for her foreign friend?*

He waited until seven o'clock, the time her flight was set to leave, then he headed home. And on the way he allowed himself a good cry. Not for the first time lately.

MALLORY HAD STARTED TO CALL TATE THREE TIMES, but each time she'd hung up before the call went through. Now she was on the plane seated next to a Middle Eastern man who looked about her age. She'd seen only one other woman on the flight, dressed in blue jeans and a white blouse that wasn't tucked in. She looked maybe midforties, and her dark hair was pulled up in a clip. She had on full makeup too. Maybe Soraya had overreacted about Mallory's need to blend. Or maybe the woman was just going as far as Dubai, a more likely scenario.

Her stomach churned with a mixture of anxiety and excitement. She'd had to pay a lot to get a last-minute flight with only one stop, but she hated takeoffs and landings.

It was going to be a long trip to Dubai, fifteen hours. Then she had a ten-hour layover before flying straight to Peshawar, which thankfully took only three hours. Abdul said he would be at the airport when she landed, which would be nine o'clock in the morning Pakistan time. And two days later, due to the time change. She was wishing she'd taken Vicky up on her offer of some pills to calm her down, but Mallory wasn't much of a pill popper and was hoping the Benadryl would be enough. She'd brought along plenty of diversions. She'd downloaded several movies onto her laptop, although she'd probably run out of battery before she even finished the second one. She had a couple of books to read, a crossword puzzle, and earbuds to listen to music on her cell phone if she was desperate. She didn't want to have a dead phone when she got there. The Houston airport had plugs for recharging, but she didn't know about Dubai.

Should have Googled it.

She'd already thought about what she'd do for ten hours there. She'd heard about the grand architecture and read that it was a popular vacation spot for celebrities, but she was arriving in the evening. And even if her flight was getting in earlier, Mallory knew she would sit safely at the gate and wait. Traveling around the city meant getting a tourist visa, not to mention worrying about getting back on time and going through security again.

She turned to the man next to her. "Do you live in Pakistan?" Normally Mallory didn't like to make small talk on a plane, preferring to read. But on a flight this long it would be nice to have at least a little conversation.

"Yes." He looked at her briefly and smiled, then he buried his head back in the book he was reading. Maybe he didn't speak good English. She let her eyes drift to the left, and she noticed the book was in English. Oh well. Maybe he'd feel like chatting later.

Fifteen minutes later she braced herself for the takeoff. As usual, she latched onto the armrests with white-knuckled hands and closed her eyes as they went airborne, popping her ears, chewing her gum, and hoping it would be a smooth flight. Despite her anxiety, she couldn't wait to meet Abdul face-to-face. And she hoped Tate hadn't been arrested for his crazy behavior.

TATE WALKED BACK INTO THE HOUSE AND FOUND HIS mother and Verdell in the living room playing a card game.

"How'd it go?" Mom pressed her lips together as the creases on her forehead formed a road map of worry.

"Well, she's gone." He shook his head. "I can't believe she's doing this. Stupid, stupid."

Mom set her cards down. "I think we'll have to quit for now."

Verdell nodded. "Thanks for playing with me, Mrs. Webber."

"Honey, you just call me Regina, okay?" She went to Tate and put a hand on his arm. "She's going to be okay, Tate. And so are you. Maybe this time apart will be good for both of you."

"We've already been apart for two weeks. And if she needed more time, she didn't have to fly across the world to get it."

"So tell me more about it, Tate. Is she going just to visit this man she's met on Skype?"

"I talked to Vicky more on the way home. She said Mallory is thinking about marrying this guy."

His mother's eyes widened, and Tate quickly held up one hand. "It's not like that, Mom. It would be a marriage in name only. The guy's daughter is sixteen and has cancer. Apparently, if he gets an American wife, it will expedite getting his daughter here for the proper care. Otherwise the process can take years." Tate shrugged. "That's what Vicky says anyway."

"Do their parents know about this?"

"Vicky said they don't, and I wouldn't want to be around when they find out." Tate glanced at Verdell, and it was clear the kid was all ears.

"How long will she be gone?" Mom asked.

"A couple of weeks." He was starting to wonder if he should get hold of Soraya. Maybe she'd have more information. Then he felt his temperature rising. Obviously, Soraya and Ismail were in on this, probably encouraging her to go.

"Well, honey, all we can do is pray for her safe return. Do you think she'll call you?"

Tate shrugged as he walked to the couch and sat down. "I don't know. I don't know anything anymore." He turned to Verdell. The kid had enough problems without adding Tate's to the mix. "What did you think about Mom's enchiladas?"

"They were really good."

This was the most normal Tate had seen Verdell act since he'd known him, which made him really start to question what kind of life the kid had been living at Chantal's. She had seemed like a nice lady, but one never knew what went on behind closed doors.

"There's plenty of enchiladas left. I put them in the fridge, though, so you'll need to microwave them."

"Thanks, Mom." He didn't really feel like eating.

"Well, I'm going to go." She turned to Verdell. "This was fun. We'll have to do it again soon."

"I had fun too."

Tate felt like he was in the Twilight Zone. He walked his mother to her car while Verdell stayed on the couch holding ET. His feline friend had never been much of a lap cat, but he'd sure taken to Verdell.

"He's a good kid, Tate," Mom said when they got outside. "But he does have some problems. What are you going to do?"

"I don't know. What all did he say to you?"

"He said that his mother's head was cut off in the boating accident, but he wasn't supposed to know that."

"Wow." Tate hung his head. "That would be hard for anyone, especially a kid his age."

"Yep. And he also said that his mother used to take him to piano competitions and recitals a lot."

"Well, he's got talent, but I don't see him doing anything with it. Maybe that's why he hates playing the piano so much. It reminds him of his mother."

"Maybe. But just be kind to him. He chose you for a reason." She leaned up, kissed Tate on the cheek, then gave a quick wave before she pulled out of the driveway.

Tate wished he didn't have to go in and put on a happy face for a troubled ten-year-old kid. But he believed that God had placed Verdell in his life for a reason. It must be part of His plan for the child.

For the life of him, though, Tate couldn't understand God's plan for Mallory.

Chapter Eleven

Mallory had never been so glad to be on the ground after a flight. Normally she got antsy about three hours into the ride. Hawaii had been a tough eight hours, but this . . . this beat anything she'd ever experienced. They'd run into a storm that produced enough turbulence for the man next to her to spill his soda. He apologized profusely, as most of it went in her lap, and despite scrubbing up the best she could in the bathroom, her colorful clothes now had a stain. That had been the only conversation she'd had with the man. He closed his book before the plane even leveled off, and he'd slept the rest of the flight. She hadn't been able to sleep, and she wasn't able to get one of her ears to pop during the landing, so she was having trouble hearing. Add a headache to the mix, and the prospect of a ten-hour layover made for a less-than-perfect start to her adventure.

The Dubai airport was amazing, though, with its multi-levels and grand architecture. Once she found the gate for her next flight, she found a seat near a row of power outlets and turned on her cell phone. She listened to Tate's message again, and for the hundredth time she reminded herself that she was doing the right thing. Then she listened to a message from her mother.

"Mallory, to say you have lost your mind is an understatement," her mother said. "But what's done is done, and all we can do now is hope and pray that you make it back safely." There was a long pause. "Your father and I love you very much."

Mallory's eyes filled with tears. She couldn't remember the last time her mother had said that. In a weird way, it almost made the trip worth it already. But she wasn't up to talking to either of her parents. She and Vicky had set up Text Plus on their phones. It was worldwide free texting when the Internet was available. And Dubai airport had it. She sent Vicky a quick message to say that she made it, and to please let their parents know that she was fine. Also Tate and Soraya.

Then she called Abdul, and he answered on the first ring. "My dear Mallory, are you in Dubai?"

She smiled. Just the sound of his voice had a soothing effect on her. "I am. I'll be here for about ten hours."

"I know. My regret for you being alone at airport. But soon we will be in each other's faces."

She grinned. She knew what he meant. "And I am really looking forward to that."

She glanced around at all the people in the airport. While

there were lots of people with dark skin and dressed similarly to Mallory, there was also a hodgepodge of other travelers. Quite a few who looked American.

"Fozia has food for your liking when you are here."

She still couldn't get over the fact that Abdul's ex-wife cooked for him and did his laundry and kept his part of the house clean. It didn't sound like any divorce she'd ever heard of. "And you're sure she is okay with me coming there?"

"Yes. Yes. The whole family has excitement about meeting you. But it is me who is most anxious. To see your beautiful person in front of me will be charming."

It was a word Abdul used a lot—*charming*. And Mallory found it to be . . . well . . . charming.

"I'm very excited to meet everyone. I'm hoping I can get a little sleep on this next flight. It's not very long. A little over three hours, I think. But any sleep would help."

"My dear Mallory. Remember that Majida does not know the news of her sickness. We want to tell her when time is right, when there is hope to say to her."

Mallory remembered Abdul telling her that via Skype. She wasn't sure she agreed with it, but she could understand his motivations and would respect his wishes.

Her heart hurt for Fozia, though. Any mother would want to be with her child during cancer treatments. But that was unselfish love, sending your child to a better place for help. She thought about her mother's message again. Maybe this trip would prove beneficial in a lot of ways.

"My dear Mallory, you travel with safety, and it is soon that I will see your beauty."

117

She smiled. "See you soon, Abdul. I can't wait."

When they hung up, she started yawning and couldn't seem to stop. She didn't want to fall asleep in the airport, though, not with her purse and laptop unattended, so she set out to find some coffee.

ISMAIL WOKE UP TO HIS EMPTY BED AFTER TOSSING and turning all night. He never slept well when Soraya wasn't there, but when he had slept he'd had awful dreams. About Mallory. Ismail was sure that his cousin had painted an idyllic picture of his life in Peshawar, but Ismail knew the truth. Abdul lived in what they considered to be a middle-class area, not far from where both men grew up. But in comparison to what Mallory was used to, it was going to be quite the shock. Ismail's parents lived in the same community, and his father had told him that they often heard bombs going off, so loud that sometimes the windows rattled. Two of Ismail's distant cousins had shamed the family when they became jihadists.

He threw back the covers and sat on the side of the bed. Visions of his childhood—things he didn't like to think about—swirled around in his mind. He'd spent years trying to forget his life there. There had been some happy times when he was growing up, but the bad was so awful that sometimes those good memories were hard to recall. Once he was dressed, he took his prayer mat from the closet and spread it out by the bed and spent the next hour praying for Mallory.

MALLORY WOKE UP STARTLED WHEN SOMEONE TAPPED on her shoulder. She gasped, latched onto her purse, and quickly looked down to see her laptop still resting against her leg.

"They are boarding the flight to Peshawar. I didn't want you to miss it if that is your destination."

It was the man she'd been sitting next to on the plane from Houston to Dubai. "Yes, I'm going to Peshawar. Thank you for waking me up," she said as she stood up and gathered her laptop.

"You are welcome," he said. His English was clear, though he was dressed in loosely fitting white pants and a long, flowing white shirt that hung past his waist.

She got the strap to her laptop situated over her shoulder. "I'd been trying to stay awake, but . . ." She shrugged, but the man was frowning.

"Do you have business in Peshawar?"

"No. I'm just going to meet a friend. Thank you again for letting me know they were starting to board." She glanced around at the empty seats nearby, then noticed there were only eight or ten people in line to board. They were all dark-skinned, and they were all men, dressed similarly to the man who had woken her up.

Her pulse picked up, and she started to recall every movie she'd ever watched about terror on an airplane. Then the true-life story of 9/11 flashed before her, and in her mind she saw the Twin Towers crumble. She knew she was being paranoid, but as she looked around, she realized that many of the men were studying her as well.

She moved toward the line, and the man who had awakened her came behind her. "What is your seat number?" he whispered.

She looked at her boarding pass and told him the number. He merely nodded. Since they hadn't spoken during the entire fifteen-hour flight, she was curious as to why he was making conversation now. When they got to the front of the line, he spoke in another language to the woman scanning the boarding passes. The airline official nodded, then scanned Mallory's pass.

Once she found her seat and sat down, she was a little unnerved to see the same man squeeze into the seat beside her. Coincidence? She didn't think so. She sat quietly, and finally he spoke.

"It is not safe for an American woman to travel alone to Peshawar. I took the liberty of telling them that we were traveling together, and since the flight wasn't close to being full, asked if we could sit together."

Mallory held her breath, unsure whether to thank this man or be terrified. She forced a smile and nodded. She was stowing her laptop under the seat when he extended his hand.

"I am Frank."

Mallory shook his hand, doubting that he'd given her his real name. "I'm Mallory," she said.

"I'm sorry I wasn't much company on that long flight. My wife insisted I take something to sleep since she knows I hate to fly."

Mallory nodded, wondering if she should be comforted that this man had a wife. "I probably should have done that. I didn't get any sleep during the last flight."

"You slept for a long time at the airport. I watched you to make sure no one bothered your purse or laptop."

She was finding this conversation to be much more unsettling than the silent flight they'd shared before. Maybe because the plane was eerily empty. And because she wasn't sure how to feel about this man arranging to sit beside her.

"Um . . . thank you," she finally said. She stared at the front of the plane, wondering who the flight attendant would be. A woman, she hoped.

"You're nervous," he said as the flight attendant—a man— walked up and down the aisle.

She turned to him. "A little. I don't like the takeoffs and landings."

He nodded. "I don't either. But you're just nervous in general." He raised an eyebrow. "I hope your friend is worth it."

She turned quickly to face him. "What does that mean?" Her hands were already clammy as she dreaded the takeoff, but now her heart was racing.

He frowned. "Peshawar is not the best place for an American woman to fly into. You should have flown into Islamabad and had your friend pick you up there."

"I'm sure it will be okay. My friend will be waiting for me at the airport."

"Very well. But with your permission, I will escort you and act as your traveling companion through security." He put a piece of gum in his mouth, then fastened his seat belt.

"That's okay. I'll be fine." Mallory took a deep breath and tried to focus on finally meeting Abdul at the airport. She reached for her earbuds, planning to avoid conversation by listening to her music. Frank had opened a book and put on a pair of reading glasses.

She thought about how her mother had left her a message saying she loved her. Then she thought about all the messages Tate had left. A knot was building in her throat, but she wasn't going to cry. She closed her eyes, chose an Eagles song, turned up the volume, and braced herself for the takeoff.

She couldn't see any of the other passengers. The two seats on the other side of the aisle were empty. The male flight attendant spoke to her in surprisingly good English when he asked her if she would like a beverage. She asked for water, and the young, dark-skinned man handed it to her without any expression on his face. This was a much different flight from the one to Dubai, and she was counting the minutes until they landed—and praying the plane wouldn't blow up on the way. It was an irrational, stupid thing to think about, but she was too nervous to even travel to the back of the plane to go to the bathroom.

She'd done the research. She knew travel to Peshawar was not recommended, but she'd had Abdul to ease her worries, and she really hadn't been all that nervous. Until now.

She wanted to talk to Frank, to ask him about the area she was going to. She wanted to know about his wife and his family. But she was having a hard time not picturing him as someone who'd been sent to kidnap her. She'd read about

Americans being targets of kidnappings in Pakistan. Abdul had told her that was only dignitaries and those of great wealth, and that the threat was no greater than in other parts of the world. Ismail confirmed that and had continued to encourage her to make the trip, repeatedly telling her what a wonderful, kind thing she was doing. He'd also said that God would look highly on this good deed.

She finally got her nerves to settle a little once the plane leveled out, but she needed more than the Eagles to distract her as she thought about all the things that could go wrong with this trip. Despite her concerns she turned to Frank. "Where in Peshawar do you live?"

He closed his book and took off his reading glasses. She glanced at the paperback. Sometimes a person's reading preferences offered a hint about the person. But Frank folded his hands on top of the book, and she couldn't see the title or author. "I live in the military district. Do you mind my asking where your friend lives?"

Now Mallory wished she hadn't asked. She didn't want to tell this stranger where Abdul lived. "I think somewhere off Charsadda Road."

Frank sighed. "He or she must be a very good friend for you to travel all this way. You must know it is not safe for Americans."

It was the second time Frank had mentioned this.

"I've checked the travel advisories. My friend says the media exaggerates about a lot of what goes on there."

Frank nodded. "That is true."

Mallory breathed a sigh of relief.

"But . . . that does not make it any less dangerous for an American there. Especially where you are going."

Mallory reminded herself this man was a stranger and not to trust him too much, but she couldn't help explaining. "I'm sure I'll be fine. I'm going there to help a friend's teenage daughter. I'm hoping to bring her back to the United States to get treatment for her cancer." In an effort to justify her actions, she added, "'Greater love has no one than this: to lay down one's life for one's friends.'" She paused, smiling. "Jesus said that."

Frank stared at her for a long time. "Yes, the prophet Jesus." He lowered his head. "Peace be upon him. There is much wisdom in his teachings. But I hope helping your friend won't cost you your life, as you just said."

"I know I'm not laying down my life. I'm just going to help her." Maybe she should stop using one of the few scriptures she knew. Save a life—yes. But she wasn't on a suicide mission.

There was no mistaking the concern in Frank's eyes, and his expression sent her heart racing. Finally, he seemed to force a smile. "I'm sure you will be fine." He reached into his back pocket and pulled out his wallet. He handed her a card. "I have friends at the consulate's office, which is very near where you are going to visit. Should you have any problems, call me and I will help you."

"Thank you. I'm sure everything will be okay." She glanced at the card, saw that he really was named Frank, and stuffed the card into her purse. This guy wasn't helping to ease the fears that were brewing—he was just making things worse. When she looked back at him, he was just staring at her, frowning. Then he put on his glasses and started reading again.

Thirty minutes before they were due to land, the flight attendant passed out the immigration forms. Mallory had to list the address of the person she was visiting, what she would be doing while in the country, and write in her father's name.

It seemed to take forever to get off the plane, and she felt like she was in the movie *Casablanca* as she descended the steep flight of stairs from the plane to the tarmac. From there she was ushered to a bus that took her to the actual airport, a facility that had zero resemblance to the architecture and beauty of the one in Dubai. It was a small building with visible armed guards from the moment she stepped off the plane.

Frank walked quietly beside her as they passed a soldier wearing tan slacks, a long-sleeved blue shirt, and a blue beret, and toting a machine gun at his side. There were a lot of others just standing around outside the airport. This didn't seem all that terrifying—she'd seen this same display in Mexico. But she was surprised to see how many military personnel were inside the airport, dressed in uniforms that resembled police officers in the United States.

The passengers were escorted into a small arrival lounge, and several lines were forming. Frank explained that there was a line for married women who were traveling with their husbands, married people who were traveling alone, one just for men and foreigners, and one for single people. He pointed her toward the single line while he walked to the line for married people traveling alone.

After an official stared at great length at her passport and visa, she was finally cleared to go get her baggage, which was where she ran into Frank again. And considering the military presence everywhere, she was thankful he was nearby. Twice he spoke to armed guards who had approached him and Mallory, and both times the men had scowled at Mallory but eventually moved on. It took over an hour for her luggage to be x-rayed, and then eventually her suitcase was opened and searched. Everything was haphazardly stuffed back inside, but one guard focused on a pair of her pink panties for much too long. Her tampons caused an unexpected ruckus, and once she got finished explaining what they were, she wasn't sure who was more embarrassed—she or the guard. She was quickly urged to move on to the next security check, and relief washed over her.

"It will cost you about two hundred rupees for someone to carry your luggage."

She turned to see Frank falling in step with her, but he also waved to a group of people walking toward them.

"Do I exchange my dollars here for rupees? Will they take American dollars?"

Frank didn't look her way but continued to wave. "Yes, you can use American money." He finally turned to her. "But you don't have much luggage. If you can handle it, I'd keep it close to you instead of paying someone."

Two men, a woman, and three children walked up to Frank. The woman eyed Mallory suspiciously. Abdul had already told her that public affection was looked down on, but based on Frank's smile, this was his family. He turned to Mallory.

"You have my card, Mallory. Safe travels to you, and I hope you enjoy your visit." He didn't smile or offer to introduce her. He just nodded and left with the group. She swallowed hard and knew she needed to find a bathroom. All the signs were in Urdu and English, just as Abdul had told her they would be.

The bathroom had a commode like in the States, but off to one side was a rectangular hole in the ground with a tank about five feet off the ground. She'd read about the Indian toilets, but she'd also read that places that were Westernized had both. She couldn't imagine having to squat over a hole in the ground, and she was wondering why she hadn't thought to ask Abdul about this small, yet significant, detail.

She walked to the passenger-pickup area where Abdul had said he would be. People stared at her, and armed soldiers snickered. Several airport employees tried to take her luggage from her. "I take to car." But Mallory held firmly to her suitcase, laptop, and purse, shaking her head and walking as fast as she could, knowing she'd feel safe once she found Abdul.

She made her way to the curb with two armed guards dressed in camouflage following her. On shaky legs, she toted her luggage back and forth along the curb as the same two men paced behind. She stopped, looked all around, and tried to calm her racing heart. The man she'd been communicating with for weeks wasn't anywhere in sight.

She fought the panic rising to the surface as she slipped on her sunglasses and pulled her purse tightly against her. Everyone who walked by stared at her. Some smirked. Her heart was racing.

Abdul, where are you?

CHAPTER TWELVE

She glanced to her left, then to her right, and fought the tears welling in the corners of her eyes. Soraya had told her that most of the men would be wearing white or blue clothing, matching pants—or *shalwar*, she reminded herself—and shirts, which were called *kameez*. She'd also said that the women would be wearing outfits similar to what Mallory had on, but more colorful. And of course the women would have head coverings. But Mallory didn't see any women except for a couple of ladies inside the airport, and they were both with men.

She was about to burst into tears when she saw Abdul walking toward her. Even handsomer than on Skype. Tall. Well built. Dressed in blue shalwar and a blue kameez. When he smiled, Mallory knew that she was exactly where she needed to be. She hurried toward him, then stopped a couple of feet in front of him, remembering that public affection was frowned upon.

"My dear Mallory." His kind eyes locked with hers. Skype did not do this man justice. "A charmed sight for me." He reached for her suitcase and then her laptop, his arm brushing gently against hers. "More beautiful than I was to know," he whispered as he motioned for her to follow him. Then she noticed two boys standing nearby, and she recognized them from pictures Abdul had sent to her. Photographs were sometimes frowned upon in their culture also, especially pictures of young girls. Abdul had asked her not to share the photos of the boys, and he hadn't sent her a picture of Majida.

The two boys got in step, one on each side of Mallory, as they all walked behind Abdul. She knew the taller boy was Waleed, the twelve-year-old, and Abdul's other son was Zyiad, two years younger than his brother.

Waleed stared straight ahead, but she could feel Zyiad's eyes on her. "Hello, you must be Zyiad." He pressed his lips together, an effort not to smile that failed him as he nodded and flashed her a toothy grin. Then she turned to her left. "And you are Waleed." The older boy nodded but kept his eyes straight ahead.

They all stopped when Abdul did, and the boys quickly scrambled to store Mallory's suitcase and laptop in the middle of the backseat and squeeze into the car on either side. There was no trunk in the small four-door, white Suzuki. Abdul got into the driver's side, which was on the right instead of the left, and Mallory walked around to the other side, opened the door, and got in the car. There weren't any seat belts, and the roads were very narrow. Everyone honked . . . continuously, Abdul included. Twice Mallory found herself reaching for the dashboard.

They traveled on the main highway for a while, and when they got to a tollbooth, it was a lot like the tollbooths in Houston, with one exception—a soldier at each entrance.

Mallory already knew that both of the boys spoke better English than their father, but Zyiad turned out to be quite the chatterbox.

"That's the university," he said when they passed by a plush green field with the college behind a line of trees. It was a gorgeous stone structure with domed rooftops. Zyiad pointed out an active-duty military fort along the way also, but it looked more like a prison to Mallory, with few windows and, not surprisingly, a huge military presence.

By the time they turned onto a side street, Mallory knew she was a long way from Houston. For a few moments it resembled parts of the French Quarter in New Orleans, with colorful side-by-side, two-story buildings with balconies. Zyiad said rich people lived there. Mallory swallowed hard. She would have expected that to be where the less fortunate lived. But another turn brought them into an area where dirty white brick and adobe structures lined both sides of the streets, with electrical lines and cables exposed and hanging haphazardly against the aged structures. The sidewalks were littered with trash, and theirs was the only car in the narrow alley. Only a motor scooter and four pedestrians shared the street with them.

"A shortcut," Zyiad said. "Father wants you to see the market."

Mallory glanced over her shoulder and forced a smile as she wondered what Abdul's home would be like. Would it fall somewhere in between this and what Zyiad referred to as the rich people's homes? She shivered as she eyed the area again, glad to turn onto a more populated street. After a couple more turns—and more honking—they were in the market district, obvious by the wall-to-wall vendors on either side of the streets. The buildings rose several stories, and people were out front selling their wares. Some of the signs were in Urdu, some in English. There were jewelry stores, toy stores, places to buy appliances, bakeries, and raw chickens hanging in a meat-market window. Mallory hoped they weren't part of the regular menu.

She had never seen such a mishmash of transportation. The cars were mostly Suzuki or Toyota Corollas, although she saw one BMW and one Lexus. Zyiad quickly pointed them out and said they belonged to *very* rich people. But there were also horse-drawn buggies, donkey carts, bicycles, buses, taxis, and enough military trucks to make her feel both safe and terrified at the same time.

They came to a point where cars could no longer get through, and Abdul turned again. He'd been quiet throughout the trip, but maybe that was because Zyiad was enthusiastically playing tour guide. Or maybe it just took all of his concentration to drive in the craziness.

"Wow. There are lots of ways to get around." She peered to her left at a brightly colored bus with graffiti on the side and then at a small cart carrying fruit, powered by a miniature donkey. "Is this where Fozia does her grocery shopping?"

Mallory wondered if she and the woman would be friendly enough to do some shopping together while she was here. At home that would have seemed unlikely, but Abdul's divorce from Fozia was clearly nothing like the divorces in America. She glanced over her shoulder to Zyiad, but he avoided her eyes and stared out the window. Waleed spoke up for the first time.

"Father does most of the shopping for food. But sometimes our mother goes to the market when we run out of something."

Mallory turned to her right and waited for Abdul to confirm what his son had said.

"Yes. It is more better for men to shop for food." He smiled, and Mallory didn't question why. She wished he would reach for her hand, add more to the conversation, or say something, anything to make her stomach stop churning. Not only was she nervous about the house she would be staying in and the food she would be eating, but she was especially anxious about being under the same roof as Fozia. Then there was the issue of the bathrooms. Would they have Indian toilets?

She yawned as she looked at her watch.

"Fozia will have food for you. Then sleep must be for you." Abdul spoke softly in a comforting tone, and Mallory's nerves settled a little.

"There is our house." Zyiad pointed to an iron gate about ten feet tall.

Abdul stopped the car outside the gate and turned off the engine. Taking his keys with him, he got out to unlock the gate. A mangy-looking white dog walked up beside him. The poor fellow was starving, his ribs exposed, and large patches of hair were missing here and there. It was hard to tell what breed, maybe a German shepherd. Mallory was no fan of dogs, having been bitten as a child, but she grabbed her chest when Abdul kicked the poor creature, hard enough that she heard the animal yelp even with the windows closed. The dog limped away, and Mallory suddenly felt sick to her stomach.

Abdul pushed the gate wide, walked back to the car, and drove them to the other side, then went through the same procedure to relock the gate. The dog was smart enough to stay about ten feet away.

"Five families live here. There is a gate at the other end too." Zyiad pointed down a long street. And sure enough, Mallory counted five houses. Three smaller homes on the left, two a little larger on the right. There was no landscaping, not even any grass. And there were no driveways, just a dirt front yard. Abdul pulled up to the first larger house on the right, a three-story structure similar to the other four homes. They appeared to be made of concrete and were all painted an off-white or tan color. Abdul's home was tan with a balcony coming out from the second floor.

"Welcome," he said, smiling as he opened the car door, then moved toward the front door of the house.

As Mallory got out of the car, dry sand slipped between her toes and sandals, and she stepped over a pile of orange rind covered in ants. She followed Abdul as Zyiad and Waleed carried her suitcase and laptop, staying a few steps behind her. She held her breath as she crossed the threshold. In the distance she could see a woman, but she was far enough away that at first she wasn't sure if it was Fozia or Majida. Then the woman drew closer, and Mallory could see that it was Fozia. Mallory knew that Abdul was thirty-nine, and Fozia looked to be around the same age. Abdul spoke to his ex-wife in what Mallory presumed to be Pashto, and Fozia responded as she eyed Mallory up and down.

Mallory told the woman that it was nice to meet her, but Fozia just nodded, then motioned to the floor, where elegant china and dishes of food were already laid out. On the floor, atop a sheet of clear plastic. Though Abdul had told her that their meals were eaten on the floor, it was still a shock. The only table and chairs were in the basement and used by the children to study or by Abdul if he was entertaining male guests. Majida wasn't allowed around any males at her age, even those who were relatives.

Fozia moved back to the kitchen area. Mallory didn't feel like they were getting off to a very good start, but she reminded herself that this was a foreign culture. Abdul had made the civility of their relationship very clear.

"Please sit," Abdul said with a smile. He spoke to Waleed in either Pashto or Urdu. The languages were so much alike— and Abdul's family was fluent in both—so she wasn't ever sure which one they were speaking. Abdul nodded toward the kitchen, and Waleed looked at Mallory.

"Father said *Ammi* is pleased to meet you too. *Ammi* means 'mother' in Urdu. *Baap* is Urdu for 'father,' but Father prefers us to talk in English unless to relatives that don't know English."

Mallory was excited to be learning tidbits of these new languages.

"And he said that after you eat, he will show you the rest of the house and your bedroom." Waleed didn't talk to Mallory with the enthusiasm that Zyiad had during their trip from the airport.

Mallory had been communicating with Abdul all this time, but she assumed it was just easier to speak through his sons, who had near-perfect English, even though it was British English. Soraya had told her that the older generations spoke no English, those Abdul's age spoke a little, but it was very important to that generation that their children know English well.

"Where is Majida?" She directed the question to Abdul, who had already taken a seat on the floor. Mallory sat down to his right, and before Abdul had a chance to answer, she heard footsteps and turned to see a young woman joining them. She was wearing a colorful kameez and shalwar like Fozia's, but neither of the women wore a head covering, and Mallory wondered if she should leave hers on or take it off. She opted for on, for now.

"There is Majida." Abdul smiled, and Majida walked to a spot across from her father and sat down.

"I am Majida. I'm happy to meet you, Mallory." She sat down next to Mallory and folded her legs Indian style underneath her.

Fozia returned carrying a tray of bread. It looked like fat tortillas to Mallory, but Zyiad told her it was called *naan*, a bread that is served at most meals. It looked like the rest of the food was already set out, forming a line in the middle of the floor.

As everyone got settled, she glanced around the house. On this first floor there were twelve-foot ceilings, beige tile on the floors, and beige walls. The couches were tan, and so were the two chairs in the room. With the exception of a red rug in the living room, there wasn't much color. Everything looked worn and old, like something she could find second- or third-hand at a resale store back home.

There were glasses at each place setting, but as thirsty as she was, she noticed no one had taken a drink, so she waited. After four more trips from the kitchen, Fozia sat down, and Zyiad said they were all going to pray now. Mallory bowed her head, but when she opened one eye, she saw that no one was bowing. Instead, each person cupped their hands together in front of them. Mallory slowly lifted her head and did the same thing. Abdul smiled.

"We do prayer in way to catch Allah's blessings. When prayer is done, we bow head then and wash blessings over face and head."

Mallory nodded, then cupped her hands in front of her. She loved this idea, and she tried to envision God sprinkling blessings down into her cupped hands. As usual, though, she didn't really know what to say to God, but she thanked Him for her safe arrival and prayed that things would go well for Majida.

And then she lost focus and started thinking about Tate. She'd tried to check her e-mails and texts in the car but had no service. She'd ask Abdul later to use his Internet to send an e-mail to her parents, Soraya, Vicky, and Tate. She knew Tate must be frantic, but in her heart Mallory knew she was doing the right thing. And this would be a life experience that she would remember forever.

She shook loose of the thoughts when everyone ran their hands across their faces and then over their heads, and she did the same thing. It was a lovely thought, this part of Islam.

"Thank you, Fozia. This looks like a wonderful meal."

Fozia nodded from where she'd taken a seat on the other side of Abdul.

The strangest thing about the meal, aside from sitting on the floor, was that there were no napkins or silverware. Everyone used their hands for scooping food onto their plates, and they ate it the same way. It was the most unsanitary thing Mallory had ever seen, but she followed their lead in an effort not to offend anyone, especially Fozia.

"This is chicken pasta mutton," Zyiad said, and Mallory had to admit, it smelled wonderful. But she couldn't help but picture the chickens she'd seen hanging at the meat market, head and all.

Unfortunately, the dish wasn't as tasty as it smelled. Mallory wasn't a huge fan of curry, plus there was enough garlic to scare away a herd of vampires. She needed to go to the bathroom but decided she would wait until after the meal. Maybe it would be like the bathroom at the Peshawar airport, with both a normal commode and an Indian toilet.

Fozia served *kheer* for dessert, which at home would be called rice pudding. Mallory thought about Ismail's advice to limit her sugar intake, but she wanted to experience everything this new culture had to offer. The pudding wasn't quite as good as at home, but it wasn't bad. When they were done,

she offered to help clear the dishes, but Abdul said he would
show her the house while Fozia cleaned everything up. Mallory
looked at Fozia for a reaction, but the woman said nothing,
and she and Majida began collecting mostly empty plates.
Except for Mallory's, which still held quite a bit.

"Does Fozia speak much English?" Mallory asked Abdul
as they walked up the stairs to the second level—fourteen
tiled steps with no handrail. Mallory was glad she was in flats.

"Fozia has good English from an aunt who learned her of
it." Abdul pointed to his left when they got to the top of the
stairs, and once they were out of sight, he wrapped his arms
around her and kissed her on the cheek. He was a larger man
than she'd envisioned, but his touch was gentle. "So beautiful,
my dear Mallory."

"It's so great to be able to hear you say that in person."

He eased her away, then cupped her cheeks. "So beautiful," he said again, and she could feel herself blushing.

"Thank you, Abdul. I can't believe we are really together,
in person."

He leaned forward and kissed her on the mouth, which
she probably should have expected, but as Tate's face flashed
into her mind's eye, she pulled away.

"I'm sorry. Too much." Abdul lowered his head.

She touched his arm. "No, it's okay. Really. I guess I just
. . . wasn't expecting that."

"You must sleep."

She couldn't argue that she was exhausted. Abdul gave her
a quick tour of the second floor, which consisted of his bedroom, her bedroom, and a bathroom in each. Mallory cringed

when she saw only an Indian toilet in her bathroom. She was thankful that there was a tank and not a bucket of water for rinsing. So she'd have to squat, but at least she could flush, and there was a roll of toilet paper.

Abdul explained that Fozia and the children resided on the third floor. He said he would show her the rooftop later, where Mallory and Fozia would be washing clothes. Mallory wanted to tell him that she'd brought plenty of clothes for two weeks, so there would be no need for washing, but he spoke up before she could.

"Sleep, my dear Mallory. Sunset will fall upon us. One hour after, the time for Isha. I will check on you to see if you might be well to pray with us." He closed the door behind him.

Mallory knew that *Isha* was the last prayer of the day. She'd heard the earlier call to prayer, the *Athan*, at the airport while she was looking for Abdul. It wasn't really spoken or sung, more of a combination. But prayer was the last thing on her mind as she fell onto the double bed covered by a colorful spread. There was one window in the room, a dresser, and a nightstand. It was a very small room, and she'd take a better look around later, but right now . . . sleep was the only thing on her mind.

IT WAS ALMOST TWO O'CLOCK IN THE MORNING WHEN Tate turned off the television in his bedroom, plugged in his cell phone, and put it on the end table by the bed. Still no e-mail from Mallory. Vicky had sent him a text saying she'd made it there safely, and Tate had thanked God a dozen times for that. He'd called Vicky about eleven to ask if she'd heard any more. Tate could tell that he'd woken her up, but she checked her phone and told him that she had no more messages from Mallory, either texts or e-mails. It was going to be a long two weeks.

He'd tried calling her a dozen times, even using the international code he'd gotten from the phone company, but his calls kept going straight to voice mail. He'd left her two messages. The first one was pretty nasty, barely coming short of calling her stupid. Then he left another one apologizing and telling her how much he loved her.

He was just getting ready to turn off the light when he heard movement in the hallway. Verdell was sleepwalking again. Tate got up, found the boy in the living room with the glassy-eyed look he'd come to recognize, and directed him back to his bedroom—a small spare room that Tate used as an office. He hadn't talked to Chantal in three days, and Tate had a feeling this was a semipermanent arrangement—at least until he called someone and found Verdell a real place to live.

But they were talking more, and Tate was starting to understand Verdell a little. The kid was odd, no doubt about it. And he'd been through a horrific set of circumstances, with his parents being killed the way they were. But there was something deep inside Verdell that seemed to want to break free but couldn't. Tate wasn't ready for him to leave just yet. And truthfully, he didn't want to be alone right now.

By now even Verdell's teachers suspected Chantal wasn't coming back, but they didn't seem interested in uprooting Verdell any more than Tate did. "He's been through so much," they all said. Tate prayed for Verdell every day, but mostly he prayed for God to give him direction about how to help the boy.

Tonight he'd said extra prayers for Mallory, and as he lay there in the darkness, he wondered what she was doing. Were she and Abdul staying up late talking? Then he realized it was daytime there. Were they eating dinner? Sightseeing? Tate doubted there would be much of that in Peshawar. Then he pictured Mallory in Abdul's arms. A disturbing vision, but he couldn't help but wonder if Majida was the only reason Mallory had embarked on such a dangerous journey.

ISMAIL FINISHED UP WITH A PATIENT, THEN HURRIED to his office and closed the door. He'd been so upset the night before, he'd almost made a full confession to Soraya at dinner. Luckily he'd stopped himself in time.

"Answer the phone, Abdul!" he yelled in a loud whisper as he paced. When the call went to voice mail, he left a message. "Call me immediately."

He finally sat down at his desk. He'd begged Allah to keep Mallory safe and to forgive him for his role in this fiasco. He'd lied to Soraya repeatedly, telling her that he had not encouraged Mallory to go to Pakistan. He couldn't help but wonder how much Mallory had said to Soraya about it. But Soraya had let it go, so Ismail would just continue to pray for Mallory. He picked up his phone and dialed Abdul's number again. His cousin answered on the second ring.

"Hello, my cousin."

Ismail sat taller. "Is everything good? Is Mallory okay?"

"Yes. We are in travel to Murree. Mallory slept for many hours yesterday." Abdul chuckled, and then Ismail heard Mallory laugh, which was music to his ears.

His cousin was smart to take her to Murree, a touristy place not far from Islamabad. He was, however, wondering what Mallory thought about the villages they had to pass to get there. What did she think about people living in make-shift dwellings in caves and tents? Abdul wouldn't have been able to shelter her from such sights along the way.

"Some villages hurt her heart," he added.

"I bet," Ismail said as he recalled those living in such filth and poverty. Then Ismail spoke to Abdul in Pashto, just in case Mallory could overhear. "You must keep her safe, Abdul."

His cousin spoke back to him in their native language. "Of course I will keep her safe."

Relieved, Ismail put his phone in his pocket and picked up the photograph of himself and Soraya that he kept on his desk. He gazed at it for a while. *My beautiful Soraya. I will keep you safe as well.*

"I'M GLAD YOU TALKED TO ISMAIL," MALLORY SAID. SHE held up her phone. "I still can't get my phone to work, but I'm pretty sure it's operator error. I'm not dialing the international code correctly, or something." She shrugged, disappointed that she hadn't been able to connect on Abdul's Internet yesterday either. He'd warned her that they had limited access. Sometimes it was due to power outages. She'd counted six since she'd arrived. Hopefully Vicky or Tate would think to check with Ismail. She'd slept for hours once she'd hit the bed, and the time difference still had her messed up.

When she woke up that morning, the boys and Majida had already left for school, and Abdul said Fozia had left for the market to pick up a few items that Abdul had forgotten. They ate leftovers from the night before for breakfast, and when Mallory looked surprised, Abdul said they did that often.

She fell asleep twice in the car on the way to Murree, but she was awake when they went through one of the nearby villages. She was shocked to see a mother standing outside a small structure that looked like nothing more than a thatched hut. The woman was pouring water over her naked baby, the sand at their feet turning to a puddle of mud. Mallory had seen things like that on television, but it was disturbing to see in person how some people were forced to live.

They spent all day together, and Abdul was exactly how she thought he would be. At times, when he could tell that she felt unsettled about something she saw, he reached for her hand and offered calming words. It had always been that way with him even when they were across the world from each other. He'd been vague about Majida, but Mallory figured he would talk to her about that when he was ready. She tried to stifle a yawn.

He'd brought two prayer mats with him, and Mallory observed prayer with him twice during the day—the *Dhuhr*, which is said after lunch, and the third prayer, the *Asr*. She didn't understand most of it because Abdul switched back and forth from Pashto to English, seemingly in an effort for her to understand, which she didn't. But she was quietly respectful.

"Will take awhile for you to be in our time," Abdul said as he turned on the headlights in the car. "Sleep, my dear Mallory."

She turned to him and smiled. "I think I will if that's okay." She hated to miss anything, but she wasn't looking forward to passing through the villages again anyway. She laid her head back against the seat. She wasn't sure how long she slept, but when she woke, Abdul said they were almost back to his house.

"Thank you for taking off work today to show me around." Abdul would be working the rest of the week, and she wondered what she would do with her time while he was away. He'd told her that the children left at a little before seven in the morning and didn't return from school until two in the afternoon. That left her with Fozia. Or did it? Was it Fozia's job to entertain her?

When they pulled up to the gate, the same dog was there. She'd already told Abdul that it had upset her to see the dog kicked. He had apologized profusely and truly seemed clueless that there was anything wrong with what he'd done. She was glad to see that this time when the dog walked right up to Abdul, he didn't react.

When they walked into the house, Majida greeted them both and said dinner was ready. The girl wasn't any more enthusiastic than Waleed, but maybe she just didn't feel well. Or maybe Abdul's two older children weren't happy she was visiting. Abdul had told Mallory in the car on the way to

Murree that they still had not told Majida about the cancer. Mallory told him that she thought they should.

Zyiad came bouncing up to them, but Waleed stayed where he was on the couch and didn't even look her way. When Mallory asked if she could help with dinner, Majida said there was no need. So Mallory sat down on the couch, deciding to take her cue from the others as to when it would be time to sit on the floor.

A few minutes later Fozia came out with a dish filled with more chicken and an overwhelming aroma of garlic. Majida carried a bowl of rice. Fozia nodded at Mallory but didn't say anything. Maybe this was normal for them, but Mallory just couldn't get past the fact that Fozia did everything a wife did—not an ex-wife. She didn't seem angry. She didn't seem happy either. She was the most expressionless person Mallory had ever met, which made her wonder how the next three days would be—three days with just Fozia, at least until the children got home, then Abdul later on.

Once they were all settled on the floor, everyone cupped their hands for prayer, then, as she'd done the day before, Mallory ate chicken and bread with her hands. She passed on the rice. She'd watched too many hands dip into it. Another custom, like the toilets, she didn't think she'd ever get used to.

An hour after sunset, everyone left the room to wash. Abdul had told Mallory that before each of the five prayers each person performs *wudu*. Feet must be washed up to and over the ankles. Hands must be washed up to midarm. And ears and eyes must be washed—in case you said a bad word or saw something that you shouldn't have. Attention was also given to the nose, in case a person breathed in anything bad.

Mallory dispersed with the rest of them and went to her bathroom. Out of respect, she washed as she knew the others were doing, the same way she'd done earlier in the day with Abdul. She avoided her eyes since she had a tiny bit of mascara on. She was wishing that everyone in the family used this type of diligent washing before a meal, not just before prayer. She hadn't noticed the children washing their hands before they ate, before everyone plunged their hands into each offering.

When she returned she participated in prayer as much as she could. Abdul had given her a prayer mat that was dark green with a red border. There was a mosque in the middle of it. It was all so different, but such a life experience.

She was excited to learn more over the next two weeks. Even though thoughts of Tate crept into her mind and she missed him, she was determined not to let it ruin her trip. This fabulous trip. Her opportunity to really make a difference.

CHAPTER THIRTEEN

Mallory woke up at one thirty in the morning, groggy but instantly aware of her surroundings. She'd excused herself shortly after dinner, bathed, and gone to bed. The cold shower had been a bit of a shock, and she didn't think she'd ever bathed and washed her hair so quickly. In Texas, September temperatures were usually in the sixties. Here in Peshawar it was much cooler. Only the first floor had heat, so she was forced to rely on a small space heater in her bedroom, and it wasn't doing much good.

She'd struggled to stay awake as much as she could the day before in an effort to get on Pakistani time, but she'd slept a lot in the car. She turned on the lamp by her bed and got her laptop. While it was booting up, she checked her cell phone. Even without actual cell service her Wi-Fi should have worked, but she wasn't getting anything, so she was hoping for better luck with her laptop.

She logged in and waited while it searched for available networks. There were two. One was password protected; the other one had a very low connectivity and showed only one bar, but she clicked on it. It took a long time to load, but she was glad when it finally connected, and she swallowed hard when she saw twelve e-mails. One from Tate. Three from Vicky. Two from Soraya. One from Regina. Two from her mother. And three junk e-mails. She clicked on Tate's first.

> Hey baby,
>
> I'm trying to understand how you could do something like this without even telling me, and I can't help but wonder what your motivations are. Is it all because you are trying to help Abdul's daughter? Or is there more to it between you and Abdul? Vicky let me know that you arrived there safely. I left messages (ignore the first one, I was mad) on your voice mail, and I've been trying to call with no luck. Hopefully you'll get this e-mail.
>
> Whatever has happened, Mallory . . . you have to know how much I love you. I've tried to give you the space you asked for, but your making this trip scares me to death. I'm worried about your safety, but I also know that I don't ever want to lose you. Please come home to me, baby. I love you.
>
> Always, your Tater Tot

She realized she was holding her breath, so she blew it out slowly. She reread the e-mail two more times before she responded.

Tater Tot,

I love you too. I'm fine. I am here because I want to help Majida, and since we were taking some time apart anyway, it seemed like the right thing to do. And—

"Ugh!" she whispered aloud when she lost the Internet connection . . . and the e-mail. She clicked to reconnect, then started over. She'd barely typed, "I love you too," when it disconnected again. After three more attempts, which took about twenty more minutes, she retyped the beginning of her e-mail and finally ended with:

We'll talk more later. The Internet here is bad, and I've lost the connection several times while writing this. Please let Vicky, your mom, and my parents know that I'm okay. And Soraya!
xo

She hit Send as fast as she could, knowing she was piggybacking on a neighbor's Internet. She knew the password-protected Internet connection was Abdul's because it was listed as Abdul0415—and she knew that his birthday was April 15. Tomorrow she would get the password from him so she could read the other e-mails, even though she wasn't sure she wanted to. She snuggled beneath the covers, nervous about the next few days alone with Fozia.

When she woke up again, it was six o'clock, and she could hear voices downstairs. She climbed out of bed and faced off with the Indian toilet, then put some clothes on and hurried downstairs, hoping to see Abdul before he left for work.

Downstairs, everyone except Fozia was getting situated on the floor. She felt a little out of place in blue jeans and a white blouse, but she sat down at the only available spot.

"Good morning," she said. She glanced around for silverware, but as before, there wasn't any. Abdul, Majida, and Zyiad gave her a cheerful greeting. Waleed finally said good morning after his father sent him an encouraging glare.

"This looks great," she said as she crossed her legs beneath her and tried to decipher what they were having. She would be ready for some good old pancakes and bacon when she got home. Pancakes. Tate's favorite. She knew Muslims did not eat pork, but she wondered about pancakes.

After prayers were said, Mallory struggled to eat the *qeema*—minced meat, Zyiad explained—but the eggs were good. It just seemed incredibly unsanitary for everyone to be scooping food and eating with their hands. Fozia still hadn't come to breakfast by the time everyone else had finished.

"Where's Fozia?" Mallory finally asked.

"She is not good feeling." Abdul stuffed a bite of qeema into his mouth with his hand, then quickly glanced at Majida. His daughter lowered her eyes right away and focused on her food. It was an odd exchange, and Mallory wasn't sure what to make of it.

Shortly after the meal, Abdul told her that he would see her at lunchtime. Majida and Zyiad gave a quick wave goodbye, but Waleed left without saying anything. The children would catch the bus to school, and Abdul's commute to work was only about five minutes. She walked them all to the door, disappointed that Fozia wasn't feeling well.

They hadn't all been out the door five minutes, though, when Fozia came out of the kitchen. She was fully dressed in a purple and white outfit, complete with scarf, which Mallory knew wasn't necessary around other women or family.

Fozia didn't acknowledge her but went straight to the dirty dishes and leftovers in the living room. Mallory walked to the area.

"I'll help you with this," she said as she squatted down and reached for a plate.

Fozia didn't argue as she stacked the metal breakfast plates and picked up pieces of leftovers off the plastic. Once she had a full stack, she headed toward the kitchen and Mallory followed. The kitchen reminded Mallory of an old kitchen from the sixties, but when Fozia started heating water on the stove, Mallory was reminded that this was not the sixties, and she was a long way from home. The fine china hadn't been laid out since Mallory's first meal with the family.

"You are very beautiful." Fozia put the dishes in the sink and turned to Mallory. "You will marry Abdul?"

Wow. The woman hadn't said two words to Mallory since she'd arrived, but she was certainly getting to the point. "I—I think so. Maybe." She paused as she stacked her plates on top of the other ones. "It would be to help Majida."

Fozia looked directly at Mallory as they waited for the water to heat on the stove, and for the first time, Mallory was able to study her. She was an attractive woman with full lips and hazel eyes. The lines of time feathered from the corners of her tired eyes, but Mallory could see that she had been gorgeous when she was younger. She was still pretty, but she just looked . . . tired.

Fozia pulled her eyes from Mallory's and stacked a few more plates in the sink. "There is nothing you can do to help Majida."

Mallory leaned against the counter. "Maybe if she can get to the United States for medical treatment, they can make her well again." Fozia's English seemed good, but Mallory spoke slowly and clearly to be sure she understood.

Fozia glared at her. Mallory wanted to say, *Look, lady, I've come to a very dangerous part of the world to try to save your daughter's life. Can't you be a little more appreciative?* But it was a thought shot from the hip, and Mallory tried to picture herself in Fozia's shoes—a woman with a very sick child, living with and serving her ex-husband, unable to accompany them to the United States for Majida's treatment. So, instead, she found a dish towel and dried the dishes Fozia washed.

When they were done, Fozia folded her arms across her chest, stared at Mallory again, and said, "I must go to the market."

"That would be great. I'd love to go with you." She wasn't sure if she wanted to spend one more minute with this woman, but until the weekend Fozia seemed to be her only chance to see anything while she was here.

"You can't go." Fozia turned to walk out of the kitchen.

"Fozia, wait." Mallory stayed on the other woman's heels all the way to the staircase, and finally Fozia turned to her and raised an eyebrow. "I'm very appreciative that you are having me in your home, and I know things are different here than where I come from. But if I've offended you in any way, I'm sorry. Abdul is a friend, and when I found out Majida was sick, marrying him seemed to be a possibility, a way to get her to the United States for medical treatment. But . . ." She shrugged, unsure what else to say.

Once again Fozia's expression was unreadable. "You can't go because it isn't safe. And if anything happened to you while you were with me, Abdul would kill me." She shook her head. "The markets aren't safe, especially for Americans."

Mallory was surprised at how good Fozia's English was. She had a slight accent, like Soraya, but barely noticeable. "Okay . . ."

Before Mallory could say anything else, Fozia hurried up the stairs, so Mallory went to her room. She tried to get on the Internet, kicking herself for not getting the code from Abdul. Whoever's Internet she'd hacked into early this morning wasn't online. She went back downstairs and waited for Fozia. About thirty minutes later, Fozia came into the living room.

"Can you give me the code for the Internet? I keep forgetting to ask Abdul, and I need to e-mail my family."

"I don't know it," Fozia said. "You'll have to ask Abdul when he comes home for lunch. If I am not back from the market by then, please serve him his lunch. It is in the blue plastic bowl on the bottom shelf of the refrigerator. It will need to be warmed up."

Mallory had seen a microwave in the kitchen. No water heater, yet they had a microwave.

Fozia moved toward the door as if the house were on fire,

and when she closed the front door, Mallory heard her turn a key in the lock. Mallory eased her way to the door and turned the knob. She was locked in. What if there was a fire?

Tate read Mallory's e-mail and breathed a huge sigh of relief. Once he'd gotten Verdell off to school—which had become a frighteningly normal part of his day—he checked his schedule to verify that he didn't have any students today. Normally he'd be bummed about that, but he'd been asked to play at three more wedding receptions over the next couple of months. Neither job was paying the ridiculous amount of money that Ismail and Soraya were paying him to play for only an hour at their reception, and which he'd repeatedly told Soraya wasn't necessary. But the less extravagant weddings were still paying gigs, and he was grateful since he hadn't picked up as many students as he'd hoped. So today he was free to run some errands, and he was meeting his mother for lunch.

"Why do you think she did this?" his mother asked after they'd each ordered a burger.

"I think it's a combination of things. We got in a fight. And she's never gotten over not being able to give her cousin a kidney when she was younger. She calls saving a life 'number one on her bucket list.'" He shrugged. "I don't know, Mom. Maybe when I wasn't looking, she fell in love with that Abdul guy over the Internet."

"I seriously doubt that's the case. But what will you do if she marries him while she's there? Even if it is just to help his daughter."

"I don't know. Vicky said she's due back a week from Friday. Maybe she's just scoping things out."

Mom let out a heavy sigh. "I just hope she returns safe and sound. From what I've heard and read about Pakistan, she has no business there."

"I know." Tate was praying constantly for Mallory to come back to him safely.

"Now, on another note, what in the world are you going to do about Verdell? You can't keep him forever."

Tate chuckled. "What makes you think I want to keep him forever?"

"I've seen the two of you together. You are a blessing in that child's life. And I think he is blessing your life in ways you don't even realize."

"How so?"

Mom reached over and touched his arm, something she'd always done when she was about to say something important, something she wanted to make sure he heard. "You haven't been as . . . uptight . . . since he's been around. You always kept such a rigid schedule, needed everything to be in perfect balance in your life." She eased her hand away and smiled. "It's impossible to live that kind of life with a child around."

Tate thought about how things had changed with Verdell there. It was true, there really wasn't a set schedule for anything. They ate when they were hungry, went to bed when they were tired, and went to ride go-karts every chance they got. It was something Tate had loved to do when he was a kid, and one of the few things that seemed to bring a little joy into

Verdell's life. He recalled the structured schedule he'd kept before. He didn't miss it.

"I guess you're right," he finally said.

"We just never know the Lord's plan, do we?"

Tate smiled. "Nope. We sure don't."

MALLORY PACED IN THE LIVING ROOM, WONDERING what time Abdul would be home for lunch. She'd tried repeatedly to use her phone and her laptop. No luck with either, and she was feeling antsier by the moment about being so far away and out of touch.

She'd been tempted to visit the third floor and have a peek at Fozia's quarters, but she'd never been a snoop in the past, so she avoided the temptation. She hurried to the door when she heard a key in the lock.

"Hey." She tucked her hair behind her ears. She'd opted to leave it long and loose this morning. Abdul said he liked it that way, which seemed ironic since women here covered their heads. "Fozia went to the market, but she told me where your lunch is in the refrigerator. And I watched Fozia walk to the gate, but I didn't see a car. Does she have one?"

"No. It is for her to travel by rickshaw." He reached for her, pulled her into his arms, and covered her mouth with his, but Mallory quickly eased away. Tate was in her heart and mind. They might be in a rut. And Tate had made her mad. But he was the love of her life, and kissing another man wasn't on the agenda.

Abdul frowned. "My dear Mallory does not enjoy?" He tipped his head to one side as he squinted his eyes in a way that Mallory had never seen.

"It's not that. It's just . . ." She raised her shoulders, then lowered them slowly. "You know . . . Tate. My boyfriend."

Abdul grinned. "Your time here is not much." He slowly nodded his head one time. "But is okay for today."

She wasn't sure what that meant. Maybe it wouldn't be okay tomorrow . . . or the next day? She wasn't worried about Abdul wanting to get too physical with her. He was a religious man, and that would go against his beliefs. But his kiss today seemed to come with a sense of urgency that she hadn't expected. She was sure Abdul was a good man, but he was still a man, and they'd shared plenty over the Internet from a safe distance. Now she was in his home.

"I'll heat your lunch for you."

Abdul nodded as he walked toward the eating area on the floor. She watched him sit down and then she headed for the kitchen. Tate would have been right behind her, his arms around her waist, distracting her from whatever task she was trying to accomplish.

She found a blue bowl in the refrigerator. There was no lid on it. More chicken. It didn't look like enough for two people, so she pulled a plate from the cabinet, dumped the contents, and put it in the microwave. It had only been heating for twenty seconds when the power went off. She waited for at least two minutes before she walked into the living room. Abdul looked up at her.

"The food only heated for about twenty seconds before the power went out. Do you want me to wait awhile to see if it comes back on?"

"My dear Mallory," he said with a smile. "My time here is forty-five minutes. Put lunch in pan on stove. Is gas."

Mallory had already noticed that there was a cooktop in the kitchen but no oven. "Of course. I should have thought of that. I'll go heat it on the stove." She went back to the kitchen and put the shredded chicken in a pan over a low flame. Since they hadn't used the pretty china since she'd first arrived, she pulled a metal plate from the cabinet. She went back to the living room and found Abdul reading the newspaper.

She sat down on the couch and sighed. "Fozia said it isn't safe for me to go to the market. Is that true?" She remembered Waleed saying that Abdul did all the shopping for groceries, so she was curious what Fozia would come home with.

Abdul folded the newspaper and set it aside. "Fozia tells you of the truth." He glanced toward the kitchen.

"It'll take a few minutes to heat up." She paused. "What places will be safe to visit while I'm here?"

Abdul sighed. "I am charmed in my heart of all Americans, but many people do not share my ideas. This is why we travel yesterday to Murree."

Mallory folded her hands in her lap. "Um . . . is that the only place I'll be able to see while I'm here?"

"Of the next week, I do not go to work two days. On that day, we can be married and go on . . ." He paused, tapped a finger to his chin, then smiled. "On our honeymoon. Right word?"

Mallory stopped breathing. "Oh . . . we don't need a

honeymoon, Abdul, since it's a marriage in name only." Abdul narrowed his eyebrows, but Mallory went on. "And . . . you know . . . I would like to talk to Majida about all of this, to hear her feelings about everything." When the creases on Abdul's forehead deepened, she said, "And we need to find out *for sure* if marriage would expedite—make it go faster—getting Majida to the United States. If not, there is no reason for us to do it."

Abdul lowered his head, then looked up at her and smiled as he tapped his finger to his watch.

"Oh. The food." She got up, went to the kitchen to check on his lunch, and stirred it. She leaned against the counter and tried not to overthink Abdul's assumption that she would wait on him the way Fozia did. If Tate had tapped a finger to his watch in an effort for her to go get his meal, Mallory would have laughed at him.

Different culture. And different men.

She turned off the burner, dumped the chicken into the bowl, and took it to him in the living room, expecting him to ask if she would be joining him for lunch, or what she was going to eat. Something.

But he raised his palms in prayer, then scooped some of the chicken in his hand and brought it to his mouth.

Mallory sat quietly and watched him, thinking how Tate would never eat in front of her without even asking her if she was hungry.

I miss you, Tater Tot.

CHAPTER FOURTEEN

After dinner Abdul asked Mallory to join him on the couch. She offered to help Fozia and Majida with the cleanup, but Abdul said there was no need. To her further discomfort, he asked Fozia to bring a tray of tea and biscuits for him and Mallory.

"I can go get the tea." Mallory moved to the edge of the couch, but Abdul put a hand on her knee.

"It is fine. Fozia will serve." Earlier in the evening he had gotten very upset with Fozia because he couldn't find the newspaper he'd been reading earlier. They'd spoken to each other in Pashto or Urdu, but Mallory had gotten the gist of the conversation. Now she sat quietly and let him enjoy it, knowing he was probably tired from work.

A few minutes later Fozia returned with a silver tray holding a small green pitcher, two white cups, and a plate of biscuits. That's what they all called them, but to Mallory they looked like Danish cookies. Fozia put the tray on the small coffee table in front of the couch.

"Thank you, Fozia." Mallory looked up at her and smiled, but as usual received a brief nod in return. She'd tried to talk to her when Fozia returned from the market, before the children got back from school, but Abdul's ex-wife seemed to have made it her mission to avoid Mallory. And as soon as the children appeared, she sent all three to the basement to study.

"This is *kawa*," Abdul said as he poured from the pitcher into both cups.

She took a sip. "It tastes a little like what we call green tea back home, but it's sweeter. It's good." She reached for a biscuit and held it for a moment, again recalling Ismail's advice. But she took a small bite. "These are good too."

Abdul folded up the newspaper and put it beside him. He crossed one leg over the other and twisted slightly to face her. "Did you find rest today?"

"I took a nap. It still feels like morning to me right now." She took another bite of the biscuit. "Oh. Before I forget again, I need the password to get on the Internet. I have e-mails from Soraya, my parents, and my sister."

Abdul smiled. "And your Tate?"

Mallory could feel herself blushing. "Yes, from Tate also."

"He is missing his Mallory?" He paused, set his cup on the tray, then stroked his chin. "What does he think of our marriage of next week?"

Mallory put her cup on the tray also, and she took a deep

breath. "I—I'm not sure. I mean, I haven't told him yet." She paused. "Don't you think that we should go to talk to someone at the embassy or consulate or whatever, someone who can tell us if our getting married will ensure a trip to the United States for Majida? I tried from home, but I couldn't find out for sure. If we go there we can get more information."

Abdul's expression turned solemn. "To tell those of authority that we do this only for Majida is crime in eyes of them. No trip at all, maybe. Must do marriage, then go to people in charge."

Mallory nodded. He was probably right. And if they got married and Abdul and Majida were denied access into the United States, at least they tried, and they would get divorced.

"We told Majida of our marriage to be, and she says you are person to save her life."

"I thought you hadn't even told Majida about the cancer."

"Fozia and me gave her word of it last night. But best to not have talks about it."

"You know, Abdul . . . if this doesn't work out, maybe I can help Majida in another way."

He raised an eyebrow.

"Maybe we could see about medical care here. I mean, I know it's expensive and you don't have insurance, but maybe I could help with that." Mallory had a decent savings, but by Peshawar standards she was wealthy. Ten thousand dollars equaled a million rupees. "We could at least check out some facilities here."

He scowled. "I will not receive your American dollars. There is no honor in that. Marriage will get Majida to your

America." He clapped his hands together. "Now we must rest. Talk more tomorrow."

Mallory stood up when he did and followed him up the stairs. At the landing, he leaned over to kiss her, but she gave him her cheek. "All will be well, my dear Mallory." He turned to go to his room.

"Abdul . . ."

He looked over his shoulder.

"Can I have the password for the Internet?"

"Of course. It is 'peace be upon him.'" He smiled.

"Are there spaces in between?"

Abdul shook his head. "Good night, my dear Mallory."

After she told him good night, she went to her bedroom, took a cold shower, and fell into bed with her laptop. She was surprised that Abdul had been so defiant about taking her money. Her father thought that anyone of Middle Eastern descent was greedy and poor. Or a jihadist. They all fell into one of those categories. He would have blown a gasket if he'd known what Mallory offered, but Abdul had certainly proven Dad's theory to be incorrect.

No matter how many times she tried, she could not get the Internet to come up. *Incorrect password*. And there was no sign of the other Internet connection she'd used briefly before.

ISMAIL FOLLOWED SORAYA AROUND LIKE A PUPPY AS she picked out items for their wedding registry. But if Soraya was happy, he would try to be happy.

"Is this the last thing to pick out in the dishes department?"

he asked, overexaggerating a smile so he wouldn't appear as bored as he was.

"The *dishes* department?" Soraya shook her head. "I know you are bored. Two more things to choose, then we are done here." She grinned. "Then we will be moving to the *bathroom* department."

"I look forward to it." He flashed her an even broader smile.

"You know . . ." She put down the vase she was holding. "Mallory has not returned my e-mail, and I'm a bit worried."

"I told you that I talked with Abdul, and all is well."

Soraya frowned and pulled her purse strap up on her shoulder. "Yes, I know. But I haven't heard from her."

"You know how the electricity is there. It goes off all the time. And the Internet is just as bad, so she wouldn't even be able to use Wi-Fi on her phone."

Soraya huffed. "Tonight we will call Abdul and you tell him to put Mallory on the phone. I want to hear her voice."

Abdul was the last person on earth Ismail wanted to talk to, but he just shrugged and said, "Yes, dear." Although it would give him peace of mind, as well, to hear Mallory's voice.

TATE TOOK THE PIZZA OUT OF THE OVEN WHILE Verdell sat patiently at the kitchen table.

"We don't eat healthy at all," Verdell observed.

From his tone of voice, a person would have thought Tate was feeding the kid ET's food for every meal. Then Tate stopped to think how many times they had gotten burgers in the last week. Three.

"Yeah, I know. I never realized how often Mallory used to cook for me. I think I kind of took her for granted."

He wondered if she was cooking for Abdul and his family. Even though she hadn't come out and said it, Tate was pretty sure she would end up marrying Abdul in order to get him into the United States with his daughter. If that happened, they'd just have to deal with it. Mallory would get a divorce, and the two of them could get on with their lives. He glanced at Verdell. Because Mallory wasn't the only one who was complicating their future. He wasn't ready to ship off Verdell. He was getting attached to the kid.

Tate cut the pizza into eighths and put it on the table and handed Verdell a paper plate. Then he sat down and bowed his head to pray, and Verdell did too.

"I don't understand why we thank God for the food." Verdell nodded toward the empty pizza box on the counter. "Red Baron made it."

Tate finished chewing, then dabbed at his mouth with a paper towel. "Ultimately, God made everything."

"That's not true."

"Why do you say that?"

"Because . . ." Verdell started to talk through his pizza. "There are seven billion people in the world, and—"

"Verdell. Swallow your food, then talk." Tate heard the words come out of his mouth. He sounded like his mother. How weird was that?

Verdell chewed for what seemed like forever, then swallowed. "There are all these people in the world, and lots of them were born at the same second on the same day in the same year. How could God make all those people at the very same time?"

"Because He's God, and He can."

Well, that didn't sound very parental. Tate smiled to himself. He recalled Verdell telling him months before that he would make a good father, which even at the time had seemed to him a strange thing for a ten-year-old to say.

"I don't believe in God."

Tate's hand halted on the way to his mouth as he watched Verdell stuff the last of his crust in his mouth, eyeing Tate, challenging him for an answer. Tate had no idea how to handle this, but one thing was for sure . . . he now knew why this ten-year-old kid was in his life.

MALLORY HELPED FOZIA CLEAN UP THE BREAKFAST area and dishes as she'd done the day before. She didn't really want to talk to Fozia, since the woman didn't seem open to any real conversation, but Fozia was her only way out of the house.

"What do you have planned today?" Mallory dried a clean dish and noticed that Fozia didn't have her head covering on.

"Cleaning." She didn't look up from the soapy dishwater as she handed Mallory a plate.

"Good. I'll help you."

Fozia looked up at her finally. "I don't need your help."

"It's a big house. We could do it twice as fast together. Then maybe go somewhere. There's bound to be somewhere around here that is safe for me to visit. I looked on the Internet, and there are several—"

"I cannot." She pulled the drain from the sink, then walked to the living room where the plastic was still on the floor. "My brother is coming for a visit today."

"Oh." Mallory wondered if Fozia's brother would be as warm and friendly as she was. "Okay." She picked up one end of the plastic and folded it toward the other end that Fozia was holding. "Abdul gave me the password for the Internet. He said it was 'peace be upon him.' But I tried and tried, and I can't get it to connect. Do you know if maybe he left out part of the password or something?"

Fozia folded the plastic up, sighing. "I'm sure I don't know."

"You don't use the Internet?"

"No."

Fozia headed toward the stairs, and Mallory knew she was wasting her time trying to communicate. The woman clearly hated her being here, no matter the reason. But Fozia was only halfway up the stairs when she stopped and turned around.

"Tomorrow I will be going to the village to visit my aunt and uncle. You can come along if you'd like."

"I'd love to. Thank you, Fozia. And my offer still stands to help you clean."

Fozia sighed and shook her head as though Mallory had asked for the moon. "The second-story terrace hasn't been washed down since the last sandstorm. It was swept but not washed. You'll find the supplies on the terrace."

"Great." She gave a little wave and smiled, but Fozia just shook her head again. Mallory had noticed that Fozia was a little more cordial when Abdul was near, but when it was just the two of them, the woman didn't seem to care what Mallory thought about her. Mallory didn't really blame her. What woman would want to serve the potential new wife?

She started up the stairs to the second story to clean the terrace. It was something to do, and she'd have tomorrow to look forward to. And maybe she would meet Fozia's brother today.

After she swept the terrace, she filled up a bucket near the faucet and began sloshing water over the area. From the second story she could see over the sixteen-foot wall that surrounded the house, but there wasn't much to look at. Barren, dry, and dirty. And chilly. She wondered what the weather was like at home.

When she heard two loud pops, at first her mind couldn't register what it was. But a series of at least ten more sent her to her knees, covering her head. She could hear the bullets whizzing by, and it seemed to go on forever. Unable to move and shaking uncontrollably, she actually screamed when someone grabbed her arm.

"Come, come, come!" Fozia had a tight grip on Mallory's arm as they both stayed bent at the waist and ran into the house.

Mallory started to cry. "It was like a gunfight! I could hear the bullets going by. Did you hear it?" She brushed away a tear, her lip trembling.

"Yes, I know." Fozia motioned for Mallory to follow her downstairs. "I will make you some tea."

Tea seemed to be the cure-all for everything, but Mallory

was sure the sweet beverage wasn't going to make her feel any better. *I just want to go home.*

"Who was shooting?" she finally asked as Fozia put a pot of water on the stovetop.

"I don't know. Militants. Radicals." She turned to Mallory and shrugged. "Maybe your people."

"My people? Like the military? I doubt that. People were just shooting in the streets." She brought a hand to her chest, hoping to calm her racing heart. "What time is it? When are the children due home? Do you have to call the school? Will they be on lockdown?"

Fozia gave her a blank stare. "This is our life. We hear and see this all the time." She frowned. "You shouldn't have come here."

"I agree! That is not a common thing to have happen where I come from. I mean, it happens. But most people would be freaked out if they saw it." She covered her ears when she heard more gunshots.

Fozia leaned against the counter and folded her arms across her chest. "When a bomb goes off or there is an explosion, it rattles our windows, even when it is many miles away." She pointed a finger at Mallory. "And *that* . . . is often your people."

"I know you're talking about the drones. Abdul and I discussed this. I don't like them either, but they have killed a lot of the bad guys." Mallory held up both palms. "I know. I know that lots of innocent people have died also. It's awful."

"One of your drones killed my four-year-old niece last year."

Mallory took a deep breath, still trembling. "Fozia, I'm so sorry. But they are not my drones. Everyone got scared when the planes crashed into the Twin Towers in New York City and the Pentagon. Since then I've just been praying for peace . . . for everyone."

Fozia handed Mallory a cup of tea, then poured one for herself. "If a plane had crashed into a building here and killed thousands of people, it would have made the news worldwide—but there would never have been such focus as there was when it happened in your homeland. Welcome to our world, Mallory. Gunshots, bombings, drones . . . we live with it daily."

"I know."

"You don't know anything."

Fozia's eyebrows narrowed, and her expression reminded Mallory of a schoolchild challenging another student to a playground fight. Despite the subject matter and Fozia's rage, Mallory found herself wanting to say, *Are you going to pull my hair now?*

"You live in a world with golden streets, a place where your government takes care of everyone, with a safety net around your little piece of the earth. We should all be you."

Mallory lost her brief moment of giddiness and put her cup on the counter. Her blood started to boil. "Streets of gold? Really? That is not how it is. We have plenty of poor people where I come from, sick people, people in crisis. And I'm no politician, but our government is as messed up as some of the others in the world."

There was a knock at the door. Fozia mumbled something

as she swept past Mallory, but it was in Pashto or Urdu. She hung back as Fozia opened the door to a man and welcomed him inside.

"This is my brother, Yunus Badr." Fozia glanced at Mallory, then shook her head as she eyed her blue jeans. "This is Abdul's friend, Mallory."

Mallory extended her hand. "Nice to meet you."

"And you." He shook her hand as he gave a quick nod, then turned to Fozia. "Four are in the hospital. No one we know this time."

Fozia let out the breath she was holding. "Alhamdulillah."

Mallory knew that phrase: *All praises are due to God.*

Fozia cleared her throat. "Mallory, I must talk with my brother. We will be in the basement. If it pleases you, help yourself to whatever you would like in the kitchen for lunch."

"Okay. Thank you." Any appetite she'd had before the shooting was gone. And there was no way she was going back out on the terrace to finish pouring water over it. "Fozia, I really need to make a phone call. I'll pay you whatever it costs, but can I borrow your cell phone?"

"I—I don't have one."

Mallory glared at her. She knew that was a lie. She'd heard Fozia on the phone before, even though she'd never seen her. Mallory wondered if Abdul knew his ex-wife even had a phone. Surely he did, since he would be the one to pay for it.

Fozia raised her chin, and she and her brother went down the basement stairs. Mallory sat down on the couch and leaned her head back. As she waited for her pulse to return to normal, she decided to go try the Internet. Again. Maybe the neighbors would be online, although she only seemed to be able to hold that connection for a few minutes at the most.

She moved toward the stairs but stopped when she realized that she could hear Fozia and her brother talking. In English. Tiptoeing closer to the basement stairs, she stood quietly. At first she couldn't make out what they were saying, but then Yunus raised his voice.

"You cannot keep this secret much longer, sister," he said. "Abdul is going to find out. There is no hiding it forever."

CHAPTER FIFTEEN

Dinner was uneventful, but tonight Mallory didn't offer to help Fozia clean up. Fozia would have politely declined Mallory's help in front of her ex-husband. But boy howdy, could the woman turn into a witch when Abdul wasn't around. Mallory could see why Abdul had divorced her. She was a bitter person.

Mallory watched her folding the plastic on the floor, wondering if she would be bitter, too, having to constantly serve Abdul . . . and Mallory. Fozia brought them tea and biscuits again. She'd already sent the children upstairs to bathe. Or more accurately, to take cold showers.

Abdul had told her that as it got colder, they would start to heat water on the stovetop for baths. Mallory had commented that it must be a long process to heat water for all of them, and he told her they shared bathwater. *Eww.* She should have known.

After everyone was gone, Abdul reached for Mallory's hand and squeezed. "I am sorry for your fear today."

She had told him earlier about the gunshots. Fozia said that they weren't that close, but Mallory heard them whizzing by. "Yeah, I'm not used to that."

"Best to stay indoors of the house until weekend. Then I will take you safe places to visit."

Mallory was looking forward to that. She didn't mention her plan of going to the village with Fozia tomorrow. She didn't want to go anywhere without Abdul anyway, knowing she would feel safer with him. Nor did she care to spend one extra minute with Fozia. And if people were having gunfights in the streets, she'd be better off just to stay inside.

For the next half hour, they chatted, and Abdul told her more about his job at the bank. She knew he was frustrated because he hadn't been promoted as he'd been promised. She felt a huge sense of relief that the marriage conversation didn't come up again, even though that was the main reason she'd made the trip. She was a little nervous about it now and constantly had to remind herself why she was doing this.

"I've tried and tried to get on the Internet, but it keeps saying wrong password. You said it's 'peace be upon him' without any spaces, right?"

Abdul nodded. "Yes. That is it. Your computer with problem maybe?" He took another biscuit.

Mallory shook her head. "No, I don't think so. I was able to connect to someone else's Internet, a neighbor I guess, but the signal strength is very weak, so I only stayed connected a few minutes at a time."

Abdul clicked his tongue. "Must not do that. Unlawful. I will check Internet tonight and report problem to you in morning."

Mallory wanted him to check it out now. She'd never felt so out of touch, and she'd been kicking herself for not setting up an international phone plan before she came here. She'd just assumed she'd have Internet and Wi-Fi.

"We must rest now." Abdul stood up and offered her his hand. Mallory was adjusting to the time change and was actually tired herself. At the top of the stairs, he kissed her gently on the cheek, then whispered, *"Allah Akbar."* He smiled when she lifted one eyebrow. "God is the greatest."

Mallory nodded as Abdul closed the door. She hurried to her laptop.

Right now—illegal or not—she was going to try to get on the Internet. And she was thrilled to see that the neighbors were online. She clicked on the unsecured link, and as before it took forever to connect. At least two minutes. She scanned her e-mails, knowing she hadn't responded to Soraya, Vicky, or her parents. Then she saw Tate's e-mail and clicked on it. Then waited. And waited some more. It wouldn't open, and then she lost connection. It took four more attempts to connect and finally open it.

Hey baby,

I miss you more than you could possibly know, and I am loving you with all my heart. I pray constantly that you are safe and well. Me and Verdell are rocking along. I'm kind of getting used to the little dude being around, lol.

Mallory smiled.

Vicky told me that you might marry Abdul in an effort to get him and his daughter here for treatment. Please tell me, Mallory, that marrying him would be just a piece of paper, that you haven't fallen for this guy? I don't want to ever be without you. Hurry home. I'll be waiting for you.

Loving you always. In my heart and prayers!

Tater Tot

Mallory started typing as fast as she could while she had a connection.

Tater Tot, I love you and miss you so much! And if all of this works out for Majida, then it's all worth it. But today I heard a gun battle, and it scared me to death. I'm fine, but it scared me. I'm writing fast so ignore any typos. Internet is bad here.

"Please stay connected," she whispered aloud.

Abdul is very kind to me, and his children are lovely. Although Majida looks like she is on the verge of tears all the time. She doesn't say much, but that's understandable. Poor girl is sixteen with cancer.

Pow! She lost it all and fought the urge to let out a word she'd only heard her father use when he was really mad. But she bit her lip, finally connected again, and started over, recalling as much as she could, then added—

> And Tater Tot . . . you are the only man for me . . . now and forever! So please know that whether I come back alone or married to Abdul, you hold my heart and you are the only man I want to be with. Please let my parents, Vicky, and Soraya know I'm okay. Gonna hit send before I lose all this. Loving you with all my heart from across the world. M.

She pushed Send and breathed a huge sigh of relief. Then she clicked on the e-mail from her mother.

> Please call us. We are worried sick. We love you, Mom and Dad

Mallory knew that was an e-mail from several days ago, and by now Vicky had told them that she was okay. She typed quickly again.

> I'm fine! My flight leaves next Friday, so I'll be home on Saturday Sept 27, Texas time. I love you both very much.

She hit Send but then sat there for a few moments as a warm feeling washed over her. She'd always known her parents loved her, but hearing them say it, even if just by e-mail and voice mail, made her want to cry.

The Internet lost connection before she could open

Soraya's or Vicky's e-mail, and she was getting tired. After a cold shower, she climbed into bed. The small space heater seemed to be working better than it had when she first arrived. Abdul had told her that during the summer months the temperature could get up to a hundred and twenty degrees. She was glad she wouldn't be here then. No amount of opened windows and fans could combat those temperatures.

It was hard to believe she'd already been here a week, but the time difference had her really messed up until the third day. She was disappointed that she hadn't had more one-on-one time with Abdul. He went to bed really early. And it would have been good for her and Fozia to be checking out backup options for Majida, maybe visiting some hospitals, getting details about what was available here. Abdul didn't want to talk about the leukemia, and he'd also asked her not to talk to Fozia about it, saying Fozia would get very upset. And Mallory didn't want to add "upset" to the woman's already bitter mood.

She fluffed her pillow and crossed her ankles, and then she thought about what kind of secret Fozia could be keeping from Abdul. Maybe she'd ask her.

ONCE EVERYONE WAS OFF TO WORK AND SCHOOL, Fozia put her hands on her hips. She was dressed in a matching flowery blue, green, and red shalwar and kameez. "Why aren't you dressed?" she asked Mallory, frowning at Mallory's blue jeans. "I said it would be safe for you to go to the village.

I didn't say to dress like an American and stand out like a human target."

"I'm not going." Mallory wanted nothing more than to get out and about, but the random gunfire had changed her mind. She was surprised that Fozia seemed upset.

"Your choice." Fozia shrugged and walked toward the kitchen.

Mallory thought about the prospect of another day alone in the house. "How do you know it will be safe?"

Fozia picked up her purse. "I don't for sure." She pulled the black bag up further on her shoulder.

"Well, you wouldn't take me to the market. How is this different?" She could still hear the gunshots whizzing past her from the day before.

"We would be going in the opposite direction. There are no military checkpoints along the way. And it would be a treat for my aunt and uncle. I hung some appropriate clothes in your closet before you arrived." She actually smiled. "I bet you've never been in a rickshaw. Might be fun for you."

Mallory had seen the clothes. And the prospect of riding in a rickshaw did intrigue her. She put her hands on her hips. "I know you don't like me. Are you sure you want to spend the day with me?"

"I'm not going to beg you. I think you would have a nice time, and it isn't a dangerous area. Well, it's not as dangerous as the market and other places. I can't say one of your drones won't fly over and kill us all, but that's always the chance we take. Stay here by yourself if you'd rather."

Mallory thought about what Abdul said the night before,

how she needed to stay inside and stay safe, but the walls were closing in on her. "I'll go change my clothes."

TATE WAS THRILLED TO GET MALLORY'S E-MAIL, AND he was feeling particularly chipper after three great lessons he'd taught today. He was enjoying a little downtime before he had to pick up Verdell from school when Chantal called.

"How is Verdell?" she asked.

There was always a part of Tate that wanted to say, *Why do you care? You dumped him.* But he never did. "He's doing good."

There was a long silence on the other end of the phone. "Well." She paused again. "Things didn't work out so well for me in Oklahoma. I'm coming back tomorrow. If it's okay with you, I'll pick up Verdell the day after. I'll be tired, and I'm not sure what time I'll get in."

Tate's heart was instantly heavy, and his mother's words rang in his ears—*You can't keep him forever.* "Uh, yeah . . . sure. Okay."

It was probably best, he figured. If Verdell left on Wednesday, he'd have Thursday and Friday to make sure everything was clean and ready before Mallory got home on Saturday.

"Okay. Thanks a lot for keeping the little guy. Did he ever get interested in the piano?"

Tate was looking around the room. Verdell's extra tennis shoes were by the front door, covered in mud. There was a spiral notebook on the coffee table that he doodled in at night, mostly pictures of bugs. Tate walked back into the kitchen and noticed a picture on the refrigerator that he hadn't seen before. A white piece of paper with one word on it in big letters. H O M E.

"Uh . . . what?" Tate gave his head a little shake. "Oh, you asked about the piano. No, he doesn't seem any more interested than he ever was. I play a lot at night, but I quit pushing him."

"Hmm . . . that's a shame." Chantal paused. "Okay. Well, see you in a couple of days."

Tate hit End on his cell phone, looked around at the clutter, and realized that he liked it. Then he walked to the refrigerator and put his hand on the white piece of paper. "I'm gonna miss you, buddy."

He forced himself not to think about it. And Mallory would be home in six days.

MALLORY STOOD BESIDE FOZIA WHILE SHE FUMBLED with the lock on the tall gate. A motorized rickshaw waited on the other side. The three-wheeled cabin cycle was multi-colored, mostly in different shades of blue with a white canvas roof and red trim. A driver sat in the front seat, and about twenty feet from the three-wheeler, the mangy dog looked on. She wished she'd thought to bring some scraps for him.

"Is this what you took when you went to the market?"

Fozia nodded as she finally got the lock to click open.

"Yes. It's good to take for short trips. When I know I must go out, I instruct the children to flag one down while they are waiting for the bus to school. They let the driver know when to be back for me."

A flicker of apprehension coursed through Mallory as she thought again about Abdul's instruction to stay safe indoors—but her sense of adventure was at full attention. She thought about the villages she and Abdul had passed on the way to Murree and wondered if that's how Fozia's relatives lived. Yesterday Fozia's brother had been dressed nicely in pressed white pants and matching long shirt. He'd been neatly shaven. He didn't look like he lived in one of the tents or caves she'd seen. But she couldn't help but wonder if Fozia might take her somewhere to intentionally freak her out.

Mallory adjusted her pink scarf over her head and around her neck and pushed the black sunglasses up on her nose. There was a chill in the air, but being covered head to toe made it tolerable.

Fozia started to push the gate open, then she hesitated and turned to Mallory. "There is one thing I must tell you," she said in a whisper. "If the driver tries to speak to you in English, pretend you don't understand him. Do you speak other languages?"

"Uh—no. I took a little Spanish in high school, but I don't remember it. Why?"

"Because if he is a bad man and he thinks you are American, he will call someone, probably in the Taliban, and they will find us and kidnap you."

Mallory went weak in the knees. "And you are just now

telling me this?" She glared at Fozia. "Are you just trying to scare me?"

Fozia sighed. "It is unlikely he is a bad man, and he will most likely only speak Urdu or Pashto. But some also know English, so just don't take the chance. If you hear him on his phone speaking English, or if he tries to talk to you in English, just pretend you don't understand and respond in some other language." Fozia rolled her eyes. "I figured you would know at least *one* other language."

Mallory dug her feet into the dirt, glared at Fozia, and whispered, "I'm not going."

Fozia grunted. "Too late. The driver is staring at us, and it would look suspicious if you go back now." She scowled. "It will be fine. Just don't talk, and keep your sunglasses on. If he speaks to you, pretend you are Italian."

Mallory walked on shaky legs alongside Fozia to the rickshaw. "That might be a challenge since I don't *speak* Italian," she said through clenched teeth.

The driver smiled, and Fozia spoke to him in Urdu or Pashto. The man looked about Mallory's age, but he was missing a couple of teeth and had a scar several inches long on his right cheek.

She climbed into the backseat with Fozia. There wasn't more than a few inches between the floor of the rickshaw and the road, and there were no doors. She wanted to ask Fozia how fast these things went, but she kept her lips pressed together and stayed quiet.

On the highway, cars whizzed past them, and Mallory was glad when the driver turned onto a dirt road away from the traffic. But their driver maintained the same speed as on the highway—which she guessed was around forty miles per hour—so the ruts in the road caused his passengers to bounce all over the place. Twice Mallory lifted off the seat enough to hit the canvas roof. It took everything she had not to scream for the man to slow down. She panicked when her sunglasses fell off and scurried to find them on the floor before they bounced out of the rickshaw. She got them on just in time to see the driver watching her in his rearview mirror. She took in a gulp of air as she pulled her eyes from his.

About fifteen minutes into the trip they turned onto another primitive road, but this one had a little more rock mixed with the sand, so they leveled out a little bit. But the road looked like it led to nowhere. Mallory began to imagine worst-case scenarios. If she were kidnapped, would she be tortured or just kept in prison for the rest of her life? Would her father send the money? She cleared that thought. Of course he would.

After miles of nothingness and dirt as far as the eye could see, Mallory finally spotted some sort of huts in the distance. She reached into her purse to get her phone so she could take a picture. She didn't even have it completely out of her purse when she felt Fozia's hand on hers, pressing down.

Dumb, dumb. She should have known that picture taking would make her look like a tourist. She glanced at the driver, who was watching her in the mirror again.

He slowed the rickshaw in front of another road that led to the huts in the distance. He spoke to Fozia again, pointing to the road. It really didn't qualify as a road, more of a walking path that led to the village.

Fozia reached into her purse, presumably for rupees to pay him.

"Are you new person to Pakistan?"

Mallory's adrenaline shot from her head to her toes when the driver spoke to her in English. She folded her hands in her lap to keep them from shaking as she spoke back to him, faking the best Italian accent she could come up with. "No English. Italiano." She couldn't fake a complexion.

But the man nodded, then held out his hand to accept the rupees from Fozia. Fozia spoke to him one last time, and Mallory thought she caught something about a return time.

It was a long walk to the village, maybe half a mile. Once again Mallory was glad to have her flats on. "Am I going to be kidnapped?" She bit her bottom lip as she and Fozia navigated the ruts in the road.

"I don't think so."

Mallory looked her way and put a hand to her chest as she stopped walking. "You don't *think* so?"

Foziai kept walking, so Mallory caught up to her. "No, I don't think so. He seemed convinced you were from Italy."

"Uh . . . how could you tell?"

Fozia didn't answer.

"So . . . people here like Italians?" Mallory took a large step over a hole.

Fozia looked at her and grinned. "More than they like Americans." Then she slowed her pace. "Also, I must tell you. No pictures where we are going. My aunt and uncle don't like that."

To Mallory's surprise, Fozia reached into her purse with

one hand and pulled out a tube of lipstick and applied it.

"That color is pretty on you. You should wear it more often." Mallory pulled lipstick out of her own purse.

"Abdul doesn't like makeup. He doesn't allow Majida to wear it either."

Mallory was quiet for a while and probably should have stayed that way, but she couldn't help herself. "Why do you let Abdul control what you do when you aren't married anymore?"

Fozia didn't seem offended at her question. "Most women in our area do not work outside of the home. In larger, more liberal cities like Islamabad, Karachi, or Lahore, it's more common. But my family is here, so I would never go to those cities. I have no skills anyway. Abdul takes care of us. He puts food on the table and pays for the children to go to the best private school in the area. He would have no honor if he didn't."

The path had gotten too narrow for more than one person to fit, so Mallory stepped back to let Fozia get in front of her. "I understand that it's his place to take care of you even though you're divorced. It's a lot different where I come from, but I get it. But things like wearing lipstick? It seems like you should be able to make those types of choices."

"There is my aunt and uncle's home." Fozia pointed to the left.

The worn structures were similar to the poverty Mallory had seen on the way to Murree. Yep, Fozia was trying to shock her, or she had set her up for something else. Mallory's stomach started to churn.

"There are a few other things you should know." Fozia stopped and faced her. She pulled her black sunglasses down until she locked eyes with Mallory. "My aunt and uncle have probably never even seen an American. They know you are coming and will go overboard to please you."

More confirmation that Fozia had a telephone. Otherwise, how would she have gotten word to them that Mallory would be coming?

"Okay . . . ," Mallory said hesitantly, before she took a deep breath.

"I do not know what you like and don't like to eat. Under different circumstances I would have gotten word to my aunt telling her anything that you don't like, because they won't want to serve you anything that isn't pleasing." She pushed her glasses back up on her nose. "Although I'm sure there is much about our food you don't like."

She sighed, and Mallory could picture her rolling her eyes behind the dark glasses.

"But it is considered rude not to eat everything you are served. For example, when you didn't eat the lamb I made the other night or the qeema for breakfast—that was very rude of you. So I'd appreciate you making an effort to eat whatever you are served."

"I'm sorry. I never meant to offend you. I'm just not a huge fan of lamb or mincemeat." She crinkled her nose. "Or curry."

Fozia laughed, which was actually nice to hear, and started walking again. "You must be about to starve then, because we put curry in almost everything."

"Yes, I know. I will do my best not to embarrass you."

"Thank you. It will most likely be a seven- or nine-course meal, so at least try a small helping of each thing."

"Seven to nine courses? Can these people even afford to feed themselves?" The moment it slipped out, she wished she hadn't said it. "I'm sorry. I really am. But it's obvious that your aunt and uncle don't live the same way as you and Abdul."

From the beginning, Mallory had pegged Abdul and his family to be middle class, based on what she'd seen and read before she arrived. At least what was considered middle class here.

She knew her eyes were bulging beneath her own sunglasses. These homes had solid brick walls, not tents like in the other villages, but the poorest areas in Houston couldn't be compared to the poverty etched out before her. There was surely no electricity, and from the looks of things, she was grateful for the hand sanitizer she kept in her purse. As much as she hated the Indian toilets, she prayed that somewhere in this tiny, run-down structure there would be one. Or did they just go to the bathroom outside?

"No. My aunt and uncle do not live like we do. Actually, they are my great-aunt and great-uncle. They are both in their eighties. They have never been out of the village, except an occasional trip to a market near here. They have a horse and cart for travel. They've never been to our home."

As shocking as all this was, Mallory still heard Fozia say "our home," which made her wonder if Fozia had any of her own money. Was it really "their" home, or just Abdul's house? Irrelevant thoughts, but there just the same. But then Mallory returned to her original fear, that Fozia didn't like her and had definitely set her up. These were probably mean relatives who would spit in Mallory's food or something.

"There is protocol. I should have mentioned this to you earlier also. First of all, do not offer to help cook, clean, or any of those other good deeds you keep tossing about."

Mallory bit her lip and waited.

"They will serve you tea or soda. Since you are a special American guest, they will most likely offer you Mountain Dew or Pepsi or *merinda*. It's a type of orange drink. Very tasty, and it will be a real treat for you if they offer it."

Mallory was still picturing herself having to squat in a hole in the backyard if she needed to go to the bathroom. And wondering if the rickshaw driver would return with the "bad people" to kidnap her.

"When they bring your drink, most likely they will bring nuts, cookies, and sweets. There will be many side dishes." Fozia grinned again. "Loaded with curry, I'm sure."

Mallory sighed, which prompted another laugh from Fozia.

"As at our house . . ."

There it was again—*our* house.

". . . there will be rice, and the main dish will be lamb or chicken."

They were getting close to one of the homes, and Mallory could see sickly-looking lambs and chickens running loose. She could smell the stench in the air. She hoped she could get through this meal. And live to tell about it.

"For dessert, they will have gone to much effort. They have known I was coming for over a week, so I'm sure they started planning the meal then. But only yesterday they learned you were coming, so I'm sure they've been scurrying this morning to make sure everything is perfect."

"How were you able to let them know I was coming?" *With your cell phone?*

"Does it matter?" Fozia waved a hand in the air. "If you are lucky, they have made homemade ice cream. That is always my favorite part of the trip. It is the best ice cream you could ever taste."

Mallory doubted that. In Texas they had Blue Bell ice cream, and everyone knew it was the best.

"Oh . . . and one more thing." Fozia slowed down. "My aunt might not eat. She will go without food if they don't have enough. Don't question that. It would be . . ."

"Rude," Mallory finished.

"Yes."

Mallory stayed beside Fozia as an old woman and a much older-looking man came toward them. Frail, thin folks. If Mallory had to eat a huge curry-filled meal that she was dreading, while this poor, hungry woman looked on . . . The man was wearing the traditional clothing Mallory had seen since her arrival, but instead of a colorful kameez and shalwar, the older woman was wearing dark blue.

Fozia greeted the couple. *"Assalamu alaikum."* Mallory knew that meant "Peace unto you."

Her aunt replied, *"Walaikum salam."*

Then a conversation ensued. The only word Mallory recognized was *American*. The couple gazed at Mallory with wide eyes, as if she were from another planet. Then they walked to her. All the way to her. Everyone has a certain area, their own personal space, Mallory would say. These people were space invaders of the worst kind, and Mallory could already smell the curry as the old woman reached out her tiny weathered hand, her nails thick with dirt beneath them. Mallory thought it was an invitation for a handshake, but instead the woman touched Mallory's arm, petting her as if she were a prized possession.

Fozia looked at Mallory. "I forgot to mention, they don't speak a word of English. Their names are Ahmad and Uzma."

Mallory nodded, allowing the woman to continue petting her arm. Uzma was smiling, and Mallory didn't think the woman had more than four or five teeth in her mouth. But there was a kindness in her eyes that was infectious, and when Mallory glanced at Fozia, the woman's eyes were twinkling in a way Mallory had never seen.

Ahmad nodded, then started into the house. The women followed him, and Uzma ushered her into the stone structure as if it were the grandest place on earth. In the middle of the room was the familiar setup for a meal, and several trays of food were already on a green rug in the middle of the cement floor. Pushed up against the wall were a cot, at least ten stacked boxes, and a pair of sandals. On the other side of the room, two chairs were pushed up against the wall and a large bird sat in a cage. There was no kitchen. It was just one room. The aroma of curry hung in the air and mixed with the smell of bird droppings.

"Nonperishable items are in those." Fozia pointed to the boxes. "They cook on a grill outside. And they have a small

generator for the icebox." She pointed to a very small refrigerator in the corner.

Mallory was sure she would have food poisoning after this
meal, but she was going to do her best to please these people.
And it turned out not to be hard at all.

The meal was laid out in courses just as Fozia had described,
and despite the heaviness of curry, everything was pretty good.
Ahmad ate, but Uzma did not. Mallory recalled what Fozia
had said, that it was rude not to eat what was offered. That
was enough of an excuse to dive into the homemade vanilla ice
cream at the end of the meal. And "pretty good" did not begin
to describe how delicious it tasted. In a poor village on the other
side of the world in a barren part of Pakistan, these people were
giving good old Blue Bell a run for its money.

"I told you," Fozia said with a smile.

Mallory smiled back at her. From the moment they'd
stepped out of the rickshaw, Mallory had watched Fozia trans-
form into a completely different person. Kind, loving, and
attentive to her elderly relatives. Mallory couldn't understand
anything they said, but Fozia did a lot of translating. The old
woman was enamored by Mallory's silver bracelet. It was a
cheap bracelet she'd picked up at a jewelry store in Houston,
but when she took it off and gave it to the woman, she'd have
thought it was a pot of gold. Uzma put it on her wrist with
tears in her eyes.

"Thank you for bringing me today," Mallory said after they
said their good-byes and were heading back down the path to
meet the rickshaw. Even though she'd had to use the bathroom
in a hole behind the house, shielded from view by two pieces of

black plastic—with chickens crowing all around her—this had been a wonderful life experience and something she would always remember.

Fozia didn't say anything. Mallory tried to chat on the way back, but Fozia's answers were clipped and she'd turned back into the bitter woman she was at home.

Too bad.

Mallory had really enjoyed the other Fozia.

CHAPTER SIXTEEN

Mallory told Abdul all about her day after Fozia and the children had gone upstairs. And after Fozia had served them tea and biscuits.

"My dear Mallory. I tell you on last night that it was not safe for you to leave house if I am not with you."

"I know. But I didn't want to stay here by myself, so when Fozia asked me, I decided to go. And I'm glad I went because I had a really nice time. It was a very different experience for me, and I'll remember it forever."

Abdul crossed one leg over the other, stroked his chin, then turned to her. "Road to village is not safe. People rob, beat, and kill." He shook his head. "Fozia was bad to take you there. What if something had gone wrong for you?"

She touched him on the arm. "But nothing did, and I really liked Ahmad and Uzma. Fozia translated, so they told me all about how they prepared the food, the animals they keep. I'm guessing you know that neither one of them reads?"

He nodded. "It must be rest time now." He stood up and offered her a hand. It was earlier than usual when they headed up the stairs, and before he said good night he planted a gentle kiss on her forehead. She'd already asked him about the Internet, and he said he didn't know why the password wasn't working. She wasn't tired at all, so she was hoping the neighbor was online so she could check e-mails.

After three hours of trying, she decided her host provider nearby wasn't going to log in. She was getting comfortable in bed when she heard footsteps, first in the hallway and then on the stairs going to the third floor. She tiptoed to her door and opened it a couple of inches, just in time to see Abdul rounding the landing and walking into Fozia's room.

She raised her eyebrows. The most unusual divorced couple she'd ever known. Maybe that was customary here, to continue to sleep with your ex.

Surprisingly, she drifted off to sleep early, and when she woke up the sun was just coming up, so she lay there awhile until she heard everyone gathering downstairs. She was excited that she and Abdul were planning to get out and do things over the weekend. But when she got downstairs, all of the children were sitting down at the eating area except Abdul and Fozia.

Mallory could smell something heating up, so she knew Fozia must be in the kitchen. She told the children good morning, then made her way into the kitchen, wondering if Fozia would have a twinkle in her eye this morning after Abdul's visit to her room last night. But when she walked into the kitchen, she was shocked to see that Fozia's eyes weren't twinkling at all. In fact, one was black and swollen. Mallory's heart thumped loudly in her chest as she gulped in a breath of air.

"What happened to you?"

Fozia began pouring glasses of milk for the kids. "I fell down." She spoke in a monotone and didn't look up.

"Wow. You're not even trying to be a good liar. Where is Abdul?"

Fozia pointed to the end of the counter. "He left you a note."

For a moment Mallory couldn't move. There was nothing worse than a man who hit a woman. She eased her way to the note, unfolded it, and began to read.

My dear Mallory,

She cringed. The endearment she'd grown to love made her feel sick right now.

It is with sadness that I must travel on these days we were to have fun times. My cousin is sick, and with honor I go to him to help his family. Please for your safeness, don't leave the house. Fozia will travel to take care of your needs.

Loving thoughts and prayers,

Abdul

"Really? He thinks he has honor but punches his ex-wife in the face?" Mallory walked up to Fozia and tapped her on the arm until Fozia looked up at her. Mallory took a good, hard look. Fozia's lip was cracked and swollen also. "How often does this happen?"

Fozia picked up two of the glasses of milk. "How often do I fall?"

Mallory grabbed one glass, knowing the fourth was for her, so she left it there. "Yes. I guess that is what I'm asking, Fozia. How often do you *fall?*"

"It depends on how clumsy I am." She shot a thin-lipped smile at Mallory, then headed to the living room. She set a glass down in front of each of the boys, and Mallory handed Majida the glass of milk she was carrying. All three said thank you, and all three avoided looking at their mother. Mallory followed Fozia back into the kitchen.

"I saw him going into your bedroom last night, but I thought . . ." She paused, biting her lip.

Fozia didn't say anything as she leaned against the counter and folded her arms across her chest. "What do you want me to say? Don't make more of this than it is."

"How can you say that? He hit you in the face!"

"Keep your voice down." Fozia scowled.

"Do you think they don't know what happened?" Mallory pointed to the living room. "Give me a break."

"Let it go. Abdul will be back in four days. I am to make your wedding outfit while he is gone, so I will be going to market later today to pick out material. Do you have favorite colors you would like for it to be? It can be however you want."

Mallory stood perfectly still and stared at Fozia. "I don't even want to be friends with a man who hits a woman. But I am here to help Majida, so I'm going to follow through and marry Abdul, for her sake. And I've already told Abdul that if our marriage doesn't get the trip to the United States expedited, I'll help you to find care here. I have money to help with her care. Not a ton of money, but it's worth a lot more here than at home." She knew she wasn't supposed to speak of the cancer with Fozia, but it was time they all put their heads together before Mallory's time there ran out and nothing had gotten accomplished.

"You are a stupid woman." Fozia shook her head.

"And you're a . . ." Mallory stopped herself and went in another direction. "I'm stupid? You're the one with the black eye and busted lip. Maybe you should rethink that."

"You have no choice but to marry Abdul. That's what he brought you here for. He will be angry if you don't."

"Uh . . . I don't know how things work here, but I have choices about my own life. I really don't care if he is angry."

Fozia's expression was somber. "You should."

TATE TOOK A DEEP BREATH. "CHANTAL CALLED TODAY." He explained to Verdell that his aunt would be coming for him in a couple of days. He tried to mask the sadness he had in his heart by saying, "But wow. We sure had a great time while you were visiting, didn't we?"

Verdell didn't reply. Tate had prayed a lot the night before. He still believed that God had put him in Verdell's life to help him heal, and also to teach him about the Lord. But if that was the case, why were things turning out this way?

Finally, Verdell looked up. "When is Mallory coming back?"

"Saturday. If you want to, maybe next week the three of us can get together. Maybe Mallory will cook something for us since I kind of failed in that department."

"I hope she had a fun vacation." Verdell folded his hands in his lap and hung his head again.

Tate's heart was breaking. Where along the line had he started loving this kid?

"I hope so too."

Verdell looked up at him. "Your kids are going to be really lucky." Then he stood up, shuffled to his room, and closed the door behind him.

Tate sat there for a few minutes before he walked into the kitchen. He poured himself a glass of water and looked at H O M E scribbled across the white piece of paper and taped to the refrigerator. "Lord, what do You want me to do?"

He waited, but there was no inner voice, no sense of the Holy Spirit. Nothing. He walked back to the living room and sat down on the couch. ET jumped into his lap. Even the cat seemed to know something was up.

MALLORY SPENT THE NEXT FOUR DAYS MOSTLY IN her room. She'd tried over and over again to talk to Fozia, but the woman avoided her at every turn. They shared meals, and that was it. Even the children were staying to themselves, mostly in the basement when they got home from school. Mallory wasn't sure how much studying was going on because she heard the boys laughing a lot. She was still hoping to bring some joy into Majida's life soon, but she had a thing or two to say to Abdul when he got home, which she knew would be any minute.

There was a knock on her bedroom door. "Come in."

Fozia walked in and straight to the bed where Mallory was sitting. She laid out a colorful outfit on the bed. "This is what you are to be married in. I hope it fits. I did the best I could."

Mallory glanced at the dress. "That's fine. But I've asked you several times over the past four days if you wanted to take me to some of the hospitals to see if we could set up appointments for Majida, and you've just ignored me. I think there needs to be a backup plan in place, just in case our marriage doesn't get things moving forward." She looked back at her computer screen, only to see that she'd lost connection. She'd e-mailed Tate once, just telling him that she was okay. She didn't mention anything about Fozia's face.

She glared at Fozia. "I need to use your phone, and don't tell me you don't have one."

Fozia glared back at her. "It is broken."

Mallory grunted. "Yeah, I bet."

Fozia left the room but returned a couple of minutes later with a cell phone in her hand. Pieces of a cell phone. She tossed the parts on the bed. "I told you. It's *broken*." Then she turned around and left again.

Mallory stared at the destroyed cell phone in disgust.

She walked downstairs, and just as she hit the first-floor landing, she heard the key in the door. Stopping at the bottom of the stairs, she folded her arms across her chest as she watched Abdul come in and close the door behind him.

"No warm welcome from my dear Mallory?" He smiled his charming smile as he set down a black overnight bag right inside the door, then stretched out his arms. Mallory walked slowly toward him, stopping a few feet short.

"I'm very upset with you for what you did to Fozia." She narrowed her eyebrows. "There is nothing worse than a man who hits a woman."

Abdul hung his head. "I am ashamed."

He sounded so pitiful that Mallory almost felt sorry for him but didn't. "You should be, Abdul. I was shocked."

After he took a deep breath and let it out slowly, he said, "Let us talk private." He motioned toward the second floor. The children were in school, and Mallory had no idea where Fozia was, but she noticed that the house had never been so clean.

Abdul opened the door that led to the second-story terrace and stepped aside so she could go in front of him. She'd promised herself she'd never go out here again, but when she hesitated, Abdul said, "It is okay, my dear Mallory."

She cringed again at the term of endearment. There were two chairs on the terrace, so Mallory sat down in one. Abdul walked to the edge and peered in all directions. "I think we are to be okay out here." He sat down in the other chair.

"It is with sadness about Fozia." He frowned, shaking his head. Then he started unbuttoning his shirt, and Mallory's heart thumped in her chest. *What is he doing?*

When he got to the bottom button, he eased the shirt

open, exposing dark hairs across a broad chest. In the middle of his chest was a fresh cut about six inches long. He looked up at Mallory with tears in his eyes. "Fozia is good woman. But she remains angry to me about our divorce. She cut at me with kitchen knife. Had I not defended myself, I feel she would have cut me more deeply and killed me."

Mallory covered her mouth with her hand as she eyed the deep cut. "You need stitches."

Abdul shook his head, then starting buttoning his shirt. "It is okay."

She sat quietly for a while. Abdul did too. Horns blaring in the distance added to Mallory's developing headache. Finally, she said, "I'm sorry I attacked you before I asked what happened. Has Fozia done anything like this before?"

"Yes. It makes me sad to say." He gazed out into the distance, a faraway look in his dark eyes. "It is the children I worry about."

Mallory thought about the way she'd heard Fozia talk to the children. She was strict with them, but she seemed to love them immensely. It was hard to picture her doing harm to them. And she'd been a totally different person when they were at her aunt and uncle's house. Her bitterness seemed directed only at Abdul.

"Have you laid eyes on Waleed's face? He has memory forever of when Fozia cut him."

Mallory had noticed the scar on the twelve-year-old's face, and Waleed was quiet, distant. "Fozia did that?"

"Yes."

Mallory thought about all the late nights she'd spent

talking to Abdul for hours on end. She really felt like she knew this man. She was relieved that he had an explanation about Fozia's face. "Of course you had to defend yourself if Fozia was threatening your life," she finally said.

"I wish that another way would have been. A violent hand is not my way."

I'm so glad to hear that. "Well, Fozia is a very bitter woman. She doesn't even try to hide it. She's worse when you aren't around."

Abdul reached over and grabbed her hand. "Please do not tell to me that Fozia has caused harm to you in any way."

"No, no. Not at all. I can just tell that she doesn't like me. That's all."

He brought her hand to his lips and kissed it tenderly. "I have missed you. And with only three days left until time for your travels, we must be married day after tomorrow. Tomorrow I must be at my work."

"I hope our getting married works."

"That is only way." Abdul kissed her hand again, and she couldn't believe that she'd thought this gentle giant to be abusive in any way. His touch was tender, and Mallory already knew Fozia was crazy bitter.

"But if we get married in two days, then what happens when I have to leave on Friday?"

"I trust that you will make travel back when time is good. When it is good for Majida and me to travel to United States. And I hear from official mouth that you might not be needed for travel back here. If I have marriage certificate and your invitation to go to United States, visa should be in order."

Mallory hoped she didn't have to come back here. She forced a smile as he kissed her hand again.

CHAPTER SEVENTEEN

Mallory overslept for the first time since her arrival, and by the time she got downstairs she knew that the children were already at school and Abdul would be at work. She was a little nervous about being alone with Fozia now that she knew what the woman was capable of. She tiptoed down the stairs, then peeked out the window. She could see the starving dog on the other side of the gate.

This trip could not end soon enough. She'd been witness to a few of her parents' fights that had gotten out of hand when she was growing up. She didn't need to be around any of that. She reminded herself again why she was here. She'd noticed that Majida had grown quieter and more withdrawn the past few days. She supposed that was to be expected since the girl had recently learned exactly how sick she was.

Mallory had spent another night with no Internet. Abdul

tried several times on his laptop to connect, and he couldn't either. She was ready to get this marriage of convenience over and done with and go home. She missed Tate more than ever. And she knew he was hurting, between his anxiety over her and his concern for Verdell.

Her ears perked up when she heard muffled voices coming from Fozia's room, but she jumped when Fozia's voice got louder.

"Shut up! Do you hear me? I will not have that kind of talk."

Mallory held her breath, but when she heard sobbing, she darted up the stairs and hurried into Fozia's room. Both Fozia and Majida looked up at her. Both were crying.

"How dare you come into my room like this!" Fozia walked toward her, and with her black eye and swollen lip, she looked like a monster. Mallory brushed past her and went to Majida. She squatted down in front of her.

"What's wrong, Majida? Did she hurt you?" Mallory gently latched onto both of her shoulders. "Tell me. Are you okay?" She'd barely said two words to the girl since her arrival, so she wasn't sure if Majida would open up to her.

"*Hurt* her? Are you out of your mind?" Fozia curled her hands into fists at her sides. "Get out of here. Leave us alone."

Mallory stood up. "I'm not going anywhere until I know that you are not going to hit Majida."

They both looked at Mallory in astonishment. Majida covered her face with her hands, but Fozia faced off with Mallory. "I do not *hit* my children. Why would you even say something like that? Majida is very upset. She said she wants to kill herself, and I will not have her talking like that. Not that this is any of your business."

Mallory ignored Fozia's glare, eased around her, and sat down beside Majida. "It's a scary thing to have cancer, Majida. I know you must be frightened, but we are going to get you the help you need, and—"

Majida jumped up and ran to her mother. "What is she talking about? Ammi, please. Is it true? Please tell me I don't have cancer!"

Fozia cupped Majida's cheeks in her hands. "No, Majida. It is not true. You do not have cancer. She is crazy."

Mallory jumped up. "Abdul said you'd told her! You can't lie to her about this, Fozia. She has a right to know."

Mallory took another step toward them, and Fozia pulled Majida into her arms. "Go away, Mallory. And stop telling Majida that she has cancer."

Mallory stood there for a moment, unsure what her next move should be. Majida buried her face against her mother's shoulder, and Fozia stroked her hair.

Then tears began to pour down Fozia's place. "Please, Mallory. I'm begging you. Leave us alone."

Mallory didn't move. Her feet were rooted to the floor. "Whatever is wrong, Majida, can I help?"

Majida lifted her face and turned to Mallory. "There is nothing you can do to help me."

Fozia was sobbing now, along with her daughter. Mallory took two steps forward. "I am so confused. What is going on?"

Fozia eased her daughter away, still sniffling. "Majida doesn't have cancer. She never had cancer. That was Abdul's way of getting you here so you would marry him. His only goal is to get to the United States, and he doesn't care how he gets there. And he won't be taking any of us."

Mallory bent at the waist and put her hands on her knees. She couldn't breathe. This couldn't be true. She recalled all the conversations she'd had with Abdul. And with Ismail and Soraya. She forced herself to straighten and put a hand to her thumping heart. "Why are you telling me now, then? And why is Majida so upset?"

Fozia ran the back of her hand against Majida's cheek, then spoke to her in Pashto. They went back and forth for a while before Fozia finally spoke in English to Mallory. "Majida does not have cancer. She is pregnant. And she knows that if Abdul finds out, he will kill her."

Mallory sat down on the bed and looked into Majida's eyes. "Is this true?"

Majida nodded, still sobbing. Mallory wasn't sure what or who to believe anymore. Had Abdul really created this awful story about Majida just to get Mallory to come here and marry him? Or was Fozia as nuts as Abdul said?

"It isn't the best of circumstances if you're pregnant, Majida. Will the boy marry you?"

Fozia grunted. "Get out of here, Mallory. You have no idea what you're talking about."

Mallory stood up and lifted her hands. "Then educate me, Fozia. Because right now, I don't know who to believe about anything!"

Majida spoke to her mother in Pashto again, and Mallory could tell by the tone of her voice that Fozia was arguing with her daughter. But Majida eventually walked toward Mallory.

"I am sorry for what lies Father might have told you. He has betrayed your trust, and for that I am sorry. But he will kill me and Anwar both when he finds out that I am with child."

Mallory thought for a few moments. "Yes, I'm sure Abdul will be upset, but he isn't going to *kill* you."

"Yes, he will," said Fozia. "It's a dishonor to our family and Anwar's family. There will be nothing Anwar's family can do to stop Abdul from killing Anwar as well."

Mallory scowled. "Are you kidding me? Or is this just another way to try to get money out of me?"

Both Majida's and Fozia's expressions suggested that they were not kidding at all.

Fozia cried some more. "Your money cannot save Majida. It is called an honor killing. It happens here, and no one will report it because it will shame the families."

Mallory felt weak in the knees. "I need a phone."

"You saw my phone. Abdul threw it when he did this to me." She pointed at her face. "He was angry at me for taking you to my aunt and uncle's."

"I need a phone," Mallory repeated. "There has to be another phone somewhere in this house."

Fozia and Majida communicated in Pashto again, and finally Majida said, "I have a phone in my room." She walked away, and Fozia said, "Abdul will do it, Mallory. He will kill my baby and Anwar when he finds out. And . . ." She paused, blinking her eyes. "He will kill you, too, if you don't marry him. I promise he will. He will have no use for you."

Mallory was sure her legs were going to give out, so she sat down on the edge of the bed. Majida returned with a cell phone and handed it to Mallory. She called an operator and got the international code for the United States, then she dialed Soraya's number. Ironically, it was the only number she knew by heart, because it was only two digits different from her own. Thankfully, she heard Soraya's voice after only two rings.

"Soraya, it's Mallory."

"Thank goodness you called. I've been worried sick! Are you enjoying your stay? Are you all right?"

Mallory's voice was cracking as she told Soraya everything, and by the end of the conversation, Mallory had tears pouring down her cheeks. "Soraya, did you know about this, that Majida didn't have cancer?" She squeezed her eyes closed and willed it not to be so.

"Oh, my dear sweet friend. It hurts me that you even have to ask that. Of course I didn't. How many times did I try to talk you out of this trip?"

"I'm sorry. What do I do?"

Soraya was quiet for a while, then said, "Mallory, you must get out of there. Catch the next flight back home. Do you hear me?"

"Yes. I'm booked to leave Friday, but I'll try to get an earlier flight. What about Majida?"

There was a long pause. "If Fozia believes Abdul to be the type of man to kill his own daughter, then he probably is, Mallory. Honor killings happen there. I had a cousin who was killed just for talking to a girl in private on more than one occasion. They hadn't done anything more than share a few kisses. The girl's father killed them both."

"I believe what you're telling me, Soraya." She looked at Fozia and Majida. "I'm just not sure who is telling the truth around here."

Fozia said something to Majida, and Majida walked to where Mallory was standing. She latched onto Mallory's free hand and pulled it to her stomach. The big baggy clothes had certainly kept her belly hidden. But there was no doubt that Majida was pregnant.

"Listen to me," Soraya said firmly. "Their fate is sealed. There isn't anything you can do. Say nothing of any of this to Abdul, and just get on the plane Friday and come home. Unless you are able to get an earlier flight. I don't think flights leave from there to here every day."

Mallory stared at Fozia and Majida. "I can't do that, Soraya. I'm not leaving her here."

"She can't go with you, Mallory! There's no time for that. You are in danger. Get out of there. If Abdul has gone to these extremes just to get to the United States, who knows what he will do."

"No," Mallory whispered.

Soraya grunted. "Get a pen and paper."

She looked at Fozia. "I need paper and pen."

Fozia hurried to her dresser and found both, which she handed to Mallory.

"Write this down," Soraya said. "This is my parents' phone number and address in Lahore. How much money do you have on you?"

Mallory didn't want to quote numbers in front of Fozia. "Enough," she said.

"Then give Majida what you can, get her out of the house, and tell her to go to Lahore. My parents will know what to do and help her get to a safe place."

"Okay. Thank you, Soraya."

"Mallory, if Abdul finds out what you've done, he *will* kill you. I do not make this statement lightly." Soraya grunted again. "I knew you never should have gone there!"

"I don't have Internet most of the time. But I will be in touch."

"Delete my numbers from this phone."

"I will. I'll be in touch when I can. And Soraya, please don't tell Tate about this. He'll just freak out."

"That is a promise I can't keep, Mallory. You are in danger, and he needs to know."

Mallory lowered her head and cried, and through her sobs said, "Tell Tate I love him. Tell him that I love him with all my heart."

"I will, my friend. Be in touch when you can."

ISMAIL THOUGHT HE MIGHT BE HAVING A HEART ATTACK. He brought a hand to his chest and paced back and forth across the living room.

"Well, I guess you could tell from my half of the conversation that Mallory is in trouble."

Ismail nodded as he continued to pace.

"I should have done more to talk her out of going." Soraya

sat down on Ismail's couch, but he continued to pace, his mind racing about how he was going to make this right. "As it turns out, Majida does not have cancer at all. Abdul is just using Mallory to get to the United States."

Ismail pushed his palm to his forehead. His head was splitting, he was sweating like he'd run a marathon, and his chest was tight. *What have I done?*

"What is wrong?" Soraya sat taller. "Ismail?"

He opened his mouth to speak but just shook his head. Soraya walked up to him, grabbed his chin, and said, "Look at me."

Ismail blinked his eyes a few times. He couldn't remember the last time he'd cried, and he was hoping he wouldn't now. "I—I . . ."

Soraya eased backward and brought a hand to her chest. "Please tell me you didn't know about Abdul's plan. Please tell me that you didn't know Majida didn't have cancer."

"No, I did not know that Majida didn't have cancer. Of course I thought she was sick."

"Then what is going on?" Soraya took a slow step closer to him, searching his eyes for the truth.

Ismail wanted to lie to her, to deny his role in this, but he couldn't seem to say anything, and he knew Soraya would take that as an admission of guilt. She took two steps back away from him as her eyes filled with water.

"No, Ismail. Please tell me that you did not have a part in this. Mallory's life is in danger."

Ismail swallowed back the knot in his throat. "I did not know that Majida didn't have cancer. I promise you that."

"What *did* you know, then?"

After taking a deep breath, Ismail told the love of his life how his father had insisted that he find a wife for Abdul. "He said it was to save Majida." He confessed that he'd encouraged Mallory to go and told Soraya about the pressure his father was putting on him.

Soraya sniffled. "Did you deliberately put Mallory in touch with Abdul?"

He nodded.

"Oh Ismail . . ." She hung her head.

"My love, please understand . . . Mallory wanted very much to save a life, and I thought she would be doing so by helping Majida. That's the only reason I introduced the two of them. I thought it would be a win-win for everyone."

She took another step backward. "No, Ismail. You let your father pressure you into doing something you knew was dangerous. How could you do this?"

"My father insinuated that if I didn't help Abdul to find a wife, harm could come to *you*."

"Mallory is my friend. How could you do this?" Soraya asked again as she dabbed at her eyes with a tissue.

"I will make things right. I will go and get her." Ismail gazed into Soraya's tear-filled eyes. "I am so sorry and ashamed, my love. But I was protecting you."

Soraya cried harder, but when he reached out for her, she stepped back even farther. "Don't touch me. You sacrificed Mallory, and that is not the way we do things, Ismail. You should have been honest with me."

"Soraya, they were threatening to hurt you. I only

encouraged her to go to protect you." He wasn't even sure how true that was. Had his father really said he'd do harm to Soraya or just implied it?

Soraya just stared at him.

"Please try to understand. I couldn't have lived if anything had happened to you."

"If Mallory dies, it will be on your conscience."

Ismail knew he would never forgive himself if that happened. He also knew that by going to save Mallory, there was a chance he would never be able to return. Never see Soraya again. "I will leave on the next flight."

"She is scheduled to be here Saturday. There is no need for you to go unless she isn't on that plane." Soraya's voice cracked as she spoke.

"If she isn't on the plane, I will go get her."

"I don't see how we can help Majida, but Mallory is going to give her some money, and . . ." Soraya brought a hand to her mouth. "Oh Ismail . . . you heard me tell Mallory to get Majida to my parents' house in Lahore! Are you going to tell Abdul and your father? They will kill her and the boy!"

Ismail didn't even try to stop the tears from sliding down his cheeks. "How can you even ask me that? You know me. Soraya . . . how can you ask me that? I would never put Majida in danger."

"Yet you had no problem putting Mallory in danger." Soraya walked to the couch, picked up her purse, and walked to the door.

Ismail was on her heels. "Soraya, let's talk about this. Don't go."

She turned to face him, her hand on the doorknob and tears running down her face. "This is not something that the man I love would do, to participate in something like this."

"I told you . . . they threatened to hurt you!"

She stared at him some more. "You are just a coward, afraid of your father. And you better hope that Mallory is on that plane. You better *pray* that Mallory is on that plane."

"I will, I will. Of course I will." Ismail could hear the tremor in his voice. "I will make this right."

"I hope you do, Ismail. But I don't want to marry you anymore."

"Don't say that, Soraya." He reached for her, but she slapped his hand away. "Please."

"You should have talked to me about this. That's what people who love each other do. You should have talked to me."

"I know, I know," he said desperately, then he begged her not to leave, begged her not to call off the wedding.

Sobbing, she looked into his eyes and said, "I can't marry you." Then she opened the door and walked out.

Ismail dropped to his knees and slammed his palms against the door.

TATE WAS GIVING A LESSON TO PARKER, HIS OLDEST student, when the doorbell rang. "Keep playing," he said, and went to see who was there. He was shocked to see Soraya on his doorstep weeping.

"Soraya, what's wrong? Is Mallory okay?"

Soraya sniffled. "I need to talk to you." She glanced toward Parker. "Alone."

Tate called over his shoulder, "Parker, keep playing. I'll be back in a minute." He walked onto the porch, closing the door behind him. "Soraya, what is it?" He felt like he couldn't breathe.

"Mallory is in trouble."

By the time Soraya finished telling him what was going on, Tate was weak in the knees. He walked to one of the chairs on the porch and sat down, his heart racing. "And Ismail knew about this?"

"He didn't know that Majida didn't have cancer. But he did introduce them via e-mail, hoping they would establish a friendship. He knew that Mallory wanted to save some-one's life. And his father was putting pressure on him to find an American wife for Abdul." Soraya sat down in the other chair.

Tate stared at her long and hard. "Did you know, Soraya?"

She shook her head. "No. I swear to you I did not. I am heartsick, Tate. I've called off our wedding because I cannot marry a man who would do such a thing." She started to cry again.

Tate took a deep breath. "Where is Ismail now?"

"At his apartment."

They both sat quietly for a while, a rough rendition of Beethoven's "Ode to Joy" continuing in the background.

"Ismail has said he will travel to Peshawar if Mallory isn't on the plane Saturday. I encouraged her to get an earlier flight if she could. But I doubt she will be able to, and it would make Abdul very suspicious if she asked for his help."

Tate shook his head. "If she isn't on the plane, I will go get her myself." His palms started sweating just thinking about being on a plane for twenty-six hours.

"Let us pray together."

Tate must have had a funny look on his face, because Soraya added, "I believe in the power of prayer, and our God—however we perceive Him—believes in us."

She lifted her palms toward the sky as Tate bowed his head, and Soraya tearfully prayed aloud for Mallory's safe return. Tate was trembling—with fear for Mallory—and with anger at Ismail.

ISMAIL RACED TO THE DOOR WHEN SOMEONE KNOCKED, praying it was Soraya. He opened the door. "Tate."

The man shoved Ismail so hard he nearly fell. He held up his palms. "Wait. Stop." But Tate drew back his fist and moved toward him. Ismail squeezed his eyes closed, knowing he deserved this and more. When he didn't feel the blow, he opened his eyes. Tate was standing in the same position, his arm pulled back, ready to swing, but he slowly put his arm at his side.

"I should beat the snot out of you, but right now you're going to tell me what to do to get Mallory home safely. Then I'll decide if I want to break your nose."

Ismail swallowed hard. "If she isn't on the plane, I will travel to Peshawar and get her."

Tate edged closer to him. "No, you don't get to clear your conscience by being a hero. If she isn't here safely on Saturday, I will go."

"You can't." Ismail had already thought about this. "I have the necessary documents already. I have dual citizenship."

"I have a passport."

Ismail shook his head. "You need a visa. Last I heard, it takes about a week to get one. And that's if all goes well and you pay extra. It usually takes up to a month."

"Then I will go apply for one today." Tate pointed his finger at Ismail. "I thought your people had honor. There is no honor in what you've done." He moved closer until his finger was close enough to Ismail's face that it caused the other man to back up. "I know you did this because you were being blackmailed. But in the process you sacrificed the woman I love. And if anything happens to her . . ."

Tate's face was blood red, and Ismail still wasn't sure the guy wasn't going to punch him.

"You just better hope she is on that plane."

CHAPTER EIGHTEEN

On her wedding day, Mallory lay in bed with a cold rag on her forehead. That was the only plan she and Fozia could come up with, to fake illness. As it turned out, she didn't have to fake it at all. She didn't know if it was the lamb from the night before, the stress, or if she'd just picked up a bug, but she was sick and running a high fever. Fozia had brought her tea and aspirin earlier, and Abdul had been in twice to check on her. Both times she'd had a hard time looking at him, but she did her best to act normal. She'd had no communication with Soraya, Tate, or anyone from home, via phone or Internet. She wasn't even able to try to get an earlier flight. The Internet wouldn't stay connected long enough. She was drifting back into a feverish sleep when Fozia walked in.

"Abdul told me that you are too sick to have a formal wedding, but he has had the papers drawn up. His father and brother are on their way to witness the signing. He will expect you to sign the papers. Then you will be married."

Mallory forced herself to sit up. "Can they do that? Is it legal?"

Fozia nodded. "And Abdul also checked all of the numbers that Majida and I have called. There wasn't anything of interest to him on my phone, but he called Soraya's number, and when he got her voice mail, he hung up. He asked me why you called her. I told him that I didn't know, but that you were probably just a little homesick. That seemed to pacify him."

"How did he check the numbers in your phone? It's in pieces. And we deleted Soraya's number from Majida's phone." Mallory took a sip of the tea that was cold now.

"He looked at our account online. I honestly don't know if it was random or if he checks it every day to see who we talk to. It's mostly just for emergencies."

"He couldn't get the Internet to work here. Did he do that at his office?"

Fozia shrugged. "I don't know. But Abdul has always been the only one to know the password. I'm certain he gave you the wrong one."

Mallory swung her legs over the side of the bed, but when she tried to stand up, she couldn't. She had a horrible thought. "Has he drugged me?"

Fozia shook her head. "Not unless he gave you something to eat or drink?"

Mallory thought back. "No. Everything I've had to eat and drink has come from you."

Fozia wanted her well, Mallory assured herself, so that she

could somehow get to a bank to wire money from her account at home—money she could give Majida and Anwar to get to Lahore. Fozia had no motive to harm her.

"And when Majida woke up this morning, her cell phone was gone."

Mallory swallowed hard. "He took it."

"We're assuming."

They were quiet, then Fozia asked, "Are you going to sign the papers? If you don't, he will be very angry."

Fozia had told her Waleed's scar came at the hand of his father. She also said she had no clue how Abdul got the cut on his stomach, but she suspected he was doing more business than just his eight-to-five job at the bank, and that his wound was the result of a transaction of some sort going bad.

Mallory wondered if he was in a drug cartel or . . . if he really was a terrorist trying to get to the United States. Fozia assured her that he was not a terrorist. She said he just wanted to get to the United States so he could set up a better life there—though she didn't believe him when he said he would then send for them all. But Mallory didn't really care what his intentions were. If she signed the papers, it was going to make it much easier for Abdul to go to the United States, whether it took weeks, months, or years. She didn't want him to have any way to get there.

"Please sign the papers, Mallory." Fozia walked closer to the bed. "Then you can get on the airplane and go home on Friday. He'll have no reason to keep you here."

"Keep me here? Would he do that?" Mallory lay back down. She'd never felt so weak and sick in her life. It felt like the flu but worse. She'd asked both Abdul and Fozia to take her to a doctor, but both of them had said it wasn't safe.

"Yes. He will keep you here until you are legally married. And if you refuse to sign the papers in front of his father and brother, it will shame him. He will be very angry. You will have to sign them, Mallory."

She wished she had a way to get online to check the rules about all this, and she was kicking herself for not doing more research. Could she marry Abdul, then file for a divorce when she got home? Would that prevent him from ever coming to the United States? She was pretty sure that her marriage wouldn't be valid at home.

"He might kill us all if you don't sign the papers."

By now Mallory knew that Fozia and all the children had been abused repeatedly at the hands of Abdul, and she was struggling on many levels. She wished she could save them all somehow, but right now she wasn't sure how much to trust Fozia. If she were in Fozia's position, she would want the man out of her life. And if Mallory signed the papers and made that a possibility, Fozia and her children would be free of his abuse. But what if Fozia was wrong about Abdul, and he was involved in something much more sinister than she thought? What harm might Abdul cause in the United States? It was all too much. But Mallory couldn't take the chance that Abdul would go nuts and kill them all, as far-fetched as that seemed.

"I'll sign the papers," she said, defeated. "I just want to get home."

"Please get dressed in your wedding clothes and make

sure that your head is covered. It would be inappropriate for Abdul's father and brother to see you like this."

Mallory could barely sit up. Getting dressed would be challenging. "Okay."

Fozia turned to leave, but Mallory called out to her. She turned around.

"Fozia? You and Abdul aren't divorced, are you?"

"No." And Fozia left. There wasn't really anything else to discuss.

Mallory recalled all the lies that Abdul had told her, luring her here. She'd sign the papers, hopefully be well enough to get to the bank tomorrow, and then she'd get on a plane back to Houston, Texas. And that couldn't happen soon enough. She would hope and pray that Abdul would never make it to the United States, but meanwhile she wasn't willing to risk this family's lives. Although Mallory couldn't wrap her mind around the fact that Abdul would actually kill his wife and children out of anger. He was abusive, yes. But a killer? Then she recalled her conversation with Soraya. If Soraya was convinced Abdul would kill his own daughter, maybe Fozia was telling the truth.

She struggled to get up, and after much effort she was dressed in the clothes Fozia had made, complete with a bright blue scarf. She looked in the mirror at her pale face and swollen eyes, sweat dripping from her forehead, then looked down at her colorful attire. It was her wedding day. And she was running a high fever.

She wanted to sit there and just sob, but when she heard voices downstairs, she knew she didn't have the luxury to let herself fall apart.

"I love you, Tate," she said aloud. Then she slowly got off the bed and made her way downstairs to become Mrs. Abdul Fahim. Wife number two.

THE NEXT MORNING SHE WAS STILL SICK. SHE HAD started vomiting after she signed her official marriage documents. Abdul had been pleasant enough in front of his father and brother, introducing everyone politely, but there was nothing wedding-like about any of it. He and Mallory had signed the papers, and then Mallory went back upstairs, undressed, got back in bed, and cried her eyes out.

Before Abdul left for work the next day, he came upstairs and said that Fozia would have to take her to the airport, that he couldn't get off work. There was no need to pretend at this point. The elephant in the room was larger than ever. Abdul had gotten what he wanted.

Mallory just wanted to go home. She politely told him thank you for her time there, not wanting to rock any boats on these rough seas. But as she packed the last of her toiletries, she thought about her time here. What an idiot she had been. This had been the worst two weeks of her life, and she wasn't going to feel safe until she was on the three o'clock flight home.

Fozia knocked on her door. "Are you ready? The children just left for school."

"Yep." She got up, found her purse, and went downstairs. They still had one thing to take care of before Mallory could leave, and once they got to the bank, Mallory had to fill out all kinds of paperwork to get money transferred from her account in Texas to an international account that Fozia was setting up. Mallory transferred ten thousand dollars from her account in Texas but was told the transfer could take two or three days. It didn't make a dent in her trust fund, but ten thousand dollars here was worth over six hundred thousand rupees, and it would be plenty for Majida and Anwar to find a safe place to live, for Majida to get prenatal care, and for them to purchase a house and get on their feet.

The plan was that once Mallory was gone, Fozia would withdraw the money. Majida and Anwar would travel to Lahore, where Soraya's parents would help them get settled. Majida would leave a note saying she was running away, and Fozia would pretend she was as shocked as Abdul.

In the back of Mallory's mind, she still wondered if Fozia was setting her up again. But there was no doubt that Majida was pregnant.

Mallory thanked the bank clerk. The man had been efficient but very unfriendly. Fozia warned her that they were not in a safe area, but they were at the opposite end of town from the bank where Abdul worked, and that seemed to make sense. Mallory just wanted to get back to the house until it was time to head to the airport. But she had a thought.

The power had gone off twice while they were in the bank, but each time it came back on right away. She assumed they would have to have generators for that purpose in a bank. She pulled out her cell phone to see if it would connect to Wi-Fi here. It did, but it was password secured.

"Sir, is there a way for me to connect to the Internet?"

The older man scowled but said, "The password is Guest."

Mallory typed it in. She hurriedly logged into her e-mail while she could, hoping to stay online for just a few minutes. She saw that she'd never opened Vicky's e-mail, but first she sent a quick e-mail to Tate.

> Heading to the airport in a few hours. I love you. I miss you. Will be home and in your arms soon. M.

She didn't know if Soraya had told Tate everything or not. If not, she didn't want to alarm him, and she really didn't have time to explain. She clicked on Vicky's e-mail. All it said was, *I love you.* Mallory smiled. There were a bunch of other e-mails, including two from her mother, but Fozia said they needed to go.

As they walked out of the bank and past the armed soldiers, Mallory's stomach churned. She tried not to make eye contact, as Fozia had instructed her, and she had on her dark glasses. Once they were in the rickshaw, her nerves settled a little, but she could feel her fever coming on again. She popped two aspirin, wishing she had something to wash them down with. The driver pulled the rickshaw into the driveway about ten minutes later, and Fozia asked him to wait.

They walked up to the door, and Fozia unlocked it. "It's eleven now. We don't have to be at the airport until one. That should be enough time for you to go through the security checks. I'm going to run to the market, but I'll be back in about thirty minutes. I have nothing for our meal tonight, and I don't need reasons to make Abdul angry. You have time for an hour nap. You'll need your strength for the long trip home."

Mallory nodded, and Fozia used her key to lock the door. Mallory went to the kitchen and poured herself a large glass of water, then she went upstairs and decided to take Fozia's advice. Her head was throbbing, but she was already packed, so she could take this time to let the aspirin kick in and rest. She coated her cracked lips with lipstick since she didn't have any actual ointment or anything else to moisten them. Then she lay down.

She woke up two hours later in a panic. It was one thirty. They should have left half an hour ago. Dizziness consumed her, but she hurried downstairs, yelling Fozia's name. When she couldn't find her, she went to the third floor, breathless by the time she got to Fozia's room. "Fozia!" She should have been back from the market way before now.

Mallory carried her large suitcase, the bag her laptop was in, and her purse down the stairs and put them by the front door. When Fozia got back, they were really going to have to hurry to the airport. She sat down on the couch, weak and hungry but trying to stay hydrated.

She stared at the front door for the next hour and a half, knowing her flight was leaving.

And she wasn't on it.

Why weren't the children home from school yet?

And where was Fozia?

Mallory spent the next two hours trying to connect to the Internet, with no luck. She was feeling worse and worse, and weak as a kitten. All kinds of thoughts were going through her mind. Had Fozia been poisoning her? Had she merely betrayed her? She couldn't have taken the money and the children and fled, because the wire transfer was going to take a couple of days. Or had the clerk been in on the gig and just said that? Had something bad happened to them all? Where was Abdul? Was Majida really pregnant?

Questions swirled in her head, but every few minutes she just laid her head against the back of the couch. She had a horrible headache, and crying would only make it worse.

She jumped when she heard a key in the lock, then pulled the blanket tightly around her shoulders. Abdul walked in first, followed by both boys, and they were all three eating chocolate ice cream cones. Majida and Fozia came in after them, neither of them with a cone in their hand. Abdul smiled broadly.

"Ice cream is always a treat," he said before taking a bite from the cone.

Mallory shivered as she moved toward them all. She glanced back and forth between Abdul and Fozia, but Fozia wouldn't meet her eyes. "I missed my plane," she said, facing Abdul. She turned toward Fozia. "Where were you? You were supposed to be here in time to take me!"

Abdul's face turned red. "All children, upstairs now!"

Majida, Waleed, and Zyiad actually ran to the stairs and took them two or three at a time. Then Abdul walked closer to Mallory. "You don't look well. But no reason to talk with badness to Fozia. It is not fault of hers that you missed plane." He paused, narrowing his eyebrows as his nostrils twitched. "We don't use a voice so loud in this house." He leaned closer to her and whispered, "Do you have understanding?"

Mallory had never heard him use such a sinister voice, so she just nodded as her eyes filled with tears. She flinched when his hand came close to her face, and he grinned before he took his thumb and ran it across her lips, smearing the lipstick all around her mouth. He put his face even closer to hers.

"We don't wear color on lips in this house." Abdul smeared it around until it was up on her cheeks. "You are clown." He laughed, then headed for the stairs as tears poured down Mallory's cheeks.

Before he reached the landing, he tossed what was left of his ice cream cone onto the floor and glanced back and forth between Mallory and Fozia. "One of you bitches clean that up." He turned and started up the stairs. Before he had gone very far, he turned around. "My dear Mallory . . ." He smiled. "You smell of sickness with your clown face, and that is not the memory I want for honeymooning night. We will wait." He shook his head. "I hope my sex of you is good for me since you have damaged and barren womb. In Allah's eyes, you are not worthy of his blessing of a child. I'd take time to think on why you of no good to your God." He grinned again.

Mallory held her breath, paralyzed. Abdul slammed his bedroom door so hard that it rattled the china in the cabinet. She looked at Fozia, and she didn't even know what question to ask first.

Fozia walked up to her and shook her head. Then she handed her a handkerchief. "I told you that you were a stupid woman."

Mallory cried harder as she wiped the lipstick from her face. "Why are you saying that?"

"You told Abdul that you have a trust account. He is never going to let you leave. The man at the bank called Abdul right after we left. He was waiting for me on the other side of the gate when the rickshaw pulled up to drop me off. He made me get in his car, drove me to the bank, and had his name added to the account so that he would have access to the money when the wire transfer goes through."

"That's illegal," Mallory said in a whisper, looking up the stairs to make sure Abdul's door was still closed. "That clerk can't do that."

"He did. And Abdul has decided that there is lots more where that came from. I know you must be thinking that I betrayed you, but I didn't."

Mallory wasn't so sure about that. "Abdul said there was no honor in taking money from me. He refused when I offered."

"Of course he did. Why dip your toe in the pool when you can jump in and swim? And now you are married to him. I told him that you put the money in the account for Majida's treatments. He still does not know she is pregnant."

Fozia walked to where the chocolate ice cream was pooling on the floor and picked up the cone. Then she looked at Mallory, blinked her eyes a few times, and said, "I'm sorry for my part in this. I knew he was setting you up by telling you that Majida had cancer so that he could marry you and get to the United States. But things have not gone as I thought they would."

There was Mallory's confirmation that Fozia wanted Abdul gone. "What about Majida?" Mallory's head felt like it was going to fall off her shoulders, it hurt so badly. "Is she really pregnant?"

"Did you not feel the baby inside of her? Yes, she is pregnant. But now no money for her."

Mallory didn't believe anyone around here. Was Fozia hinting that Mallory should somehow give her more money? She brushed past her, picked up her laptop and her purse, knowing that was all she could manage and get herself upstairs too. But Fozia went and got the big suitcase and carried it up for her. She set it by Mallory's door, then went to her room on the next floor.

Mallory pulled her suitcase into her room and closed the door. Then she fell onto the bed and sobbed.

As sick as she was, she opened her computer. *Please, God, please. Let it connect.* It wasn't like she'd never prayed before, but right now she needed that "relationship" with God, the closeness that Tate talked about, and an abundance of faith that her Maker would hear her. She didn't know who had it right?—Lutherans, Catholics, Baptists, Methodists . . . or was it the Muslims, the Jews . . . or another group?

"Greater love has no one than this: to lay down one's life for one's friends." Is that what she'd ultimately have done if Abdul killed her? Would it assure her a place in heaven or paradise? But whom had she saved? *No one.* She prepared for fear to overtake her, but instead a feeling started to wrap around her, something she didn't quite understand, but she knew what it was. She'd heard Tate talk about it. Everything in her being told her to embrace it and drop to her knees, so she did.

And she begged the Lord, her God, to get her home.

CHAPTER NINETEEN

Tate pulled into his driveway after spending three hours at the airport looking for Mallory. No one would confirm that she was or wasn't on the plane—he'd been told it was against the rules to reveal whether a passenger made a flight. But he'd stayed around, wondering if maybe she'd been detained at customs. He had texted, sent e-mails, and called. Nothing. He was trying not to panic. Maybe she had taken a later flight. She knew he'd be worried, so hopefully she would find a way to get in touch with him. He wanted to get on a plane at once to go get her. But no visa, no trip to Pakistan. And the officials where he'd applied for the visa confirmed what Ismail said. It could take a week or a month. And without an actual invitation to travel there, Tate wasn't even sure he would be issued a visa.

He walked into the house, sat down on the couch, and tried to figure out his next plan of action. He'd already texted

Soraya and Vicky that Mallory wasn't on the plane. They'd all agreed not to say anything to Mallory's parents yet. Tate was doing enough worrying for all of them, but Mallory's dad had a bad heart.

Tate hadn't been home five minutes when there was a knock at the door. He found Chantal and Verdell standing on the porch.

"Hey, buddy." Tate tried to muster up as much enthusiasm as he could. "What's up?"

"Can you keep Verdell for a day or two?"

It was the worst possible time for Chantal to pull this, but when Tate started to tell her that, he looked down at Verdell, and he just couldn't.

"Sure," he said, and opened the door for Verdell to go in. "You can watch TV if you want to, Verdell. I need to take care of a few things on my computer, okay?"

Chantal took a step backward and gave a little wave. "Thank you, Tate. He loves staying with you." She hurried to her car, probably worried Tate would change his mind.

"I think Aunt Chantal is going back to Oklahoma," Verdell said after Tate had closed the door.

Tate nodded as he got on the Internet. That probably meant more than a day or two, but he couldn't focus on Verdell right now. He couldn't even keep his thoughts straight. He pulled up his e-mail, and his heart flipped in his chest when he saw an e-mail from Mallory. In the subject line in all caps it said, "HELP." Tate's heart started to pound as he read.

I'm in trouble. I married Abdul. He made me miss my plane. I think he is going to try to keep me here. I just looked in my purse for the first time in a couple of days. My credit cards are gone and so is the little bit of cash I had. I have no way to get out of here or to book a flight home. I'll lose connection soon. I don't know what to do.

And that was all. Tate stood up and paced. Consulate? Embassy? Who should he call? Did Mallory register with any of those places?

"What's wrong?" Verdell looked up from where he was sitting on the floor watching television.

"I gotta think, Verdell!" Tate took some deep breaths and lowered his voice. "Just give me a minute, okay?"

Verdell turned back around.

"Sorry, buddy. I'm just having a problem right now. Okay?"

He didn't look at Tate, just nodded.

Tate couldn't think. Maybe he should call Soraya. Vicky. Mallory's parents. He got back on the Internet and found the phone number to the US consulate in Peshawar. He was getting ready to dial the number when his phone rang. Les Stephens. Tate didn't have time to deal with Les or anything else to do with jobs or teaching, so he let it go to voice mail.

He dialed the number to the consulate, but it wouldn't connect, something about an international code, so he Googled how to call Pakistan from the United States. Once he had the international code, he called again, but before anyone even answered, he hung up. "Idiot! Idiot!" He didn't even have the address where Mallory was staying. He dialed Soraya's number, but no answer. Then he dialed Ismail's number, the last person he wanted to talk to right now. No answer.

"Ismail, it's Tate. Call me back. I need Abdul's address. Call me back!"

He sat down on the couch, put his elbows on his knees, and covered his face with his hands. Mallory's parents had money. Maybe they could do more than he could. He called Vicky, and she answered on the first ring.

"Did you hear from her?"

Tate didn't want to lie, but he didn't want to freak her out either.

"I got an e-mail. She's scared. I'm waiting to hear from Ismail or Soraya to get the address where she's staying. Did she give it to you?"

"No. My mom is going crazy, though, because Mallory wasn't on the plane. I finally had to tell her. I checked with Nelson since he's a cop, and he said we need to call the consulate. Do you want me to do that?"

"No, I just found the number. I need Abdul's address, though."

"Mom lied to Dad and told him Mallory booked a later flight. Apparently at his doctor's appointment last week they told him that he's had a couple of small strokes, and Mom doesn't want him worrying any more than he has to." Vicky paused. "I don't know why she's just now telling me this. But just tell me what to do, Tate."

"Let me make some calls. Vicky, I already applied for a

visa. I don't know if I'm going to be able to get it, how long it will take, or anything else. But I will go get her if I can."

"I know you don't fly."

He swallowed hard. "I will get her home."

He told Vicky that he would keep her informed, then tried calling both Ismail and Soraya again. Neither answered. He left another message on Ismail's voice mail.

"I got an e-mail from Mallory, and she is in real trouble over there. Ismail, you call me back with that address, or I will come find you and finish what I should have done when I was there!"

Tate tossed his phone onto the coffee table. He'd had one fight in his entire life, when he was in high school, and it had been self-defense. He hated violence, but he'd never wanted to hit someone so badly in his entire life. He cradled his head in his hands again. When the television went silent, he looked up to see that Verdell had turned it off and was watching him.

Verdell sat down beside him, put his hand on his leg, and said, "Maybe we need to pray."

Tate uncovered his face and looked at Verdell. "I thought you didn't believe in God."

Verdell shrugged. "But you do."

Tate just nodded. He prayed silently, afraid he might cry at any moment. "I already said a prayer." He had been praying. For days. And things were just getting worse. *Please, God, don't let anything happen to her.*

"What's wrong with Mallory?"

Tate took a deep breath, wondering if he should call his

mother to come pick up Verdell before he snapped at the kid again. He needed to let her know what was going on anyway, but she was still at work, and he was hoping he could call when he had more information. He'd already decided that he was going to give Ismail thirty more minutes, then he'd load Verdell up and go look for him.

He jumped when the phone rang, and it was Ismail.

"Here is the address."

Tate picked up a pen and scribbled the address on the back of a piece of music on the coffee table.

"I didn't want to call my father or anyone over there and alert them that someone might be coming for Mallory, so I had to find the address and—"

"You better hope nothing happens to her!" Tate hit End and threw the phone down on the couch. He found the number to the consulate again, grabbed up the phone, and dialed.

Verdell stayed right there, his eyes never leaving Tate.

"I'm calling from the United States, and I have a friend in trouble there. I need to know what to do."

A man who spoke poor English said, "Your friend come to consulate."

"What? She's being held against her will. I have the address."

"She must come to consulate for help."

"She can't get to the consulate. I need to give you the address so that someone can go get her!" Tate knew his voice was getting louder, so he took another deep breath. "Please. I'll give you the address."

"One moment. I transfer you."

Tate resisted the urge to hurl the phone across the room as he tapped his bare foot and waited. Finally, a woman answered the phone, and she didn't have an accent. Tate explained what was going on.

"Mr. Webber, I'm going to do everything I can to help you. I'm going to give you the phone number for a woman named Cynthia Stratton, and—"

Tate bolted off the couch. "No, please don't pass me off to someone else. I need to give you the address so that someone can go get her. If I need to buy her a ticket home, just tell me. But please, someone has to go get her. The man she's with is dangerous."

"Mr. Webber, I need you to listen to me. Ms. Stratton is with the Department of State, the Bureau of Consular Affairs in the office of Overseas Citizens Services. She's in Washington, DC."

Tate slammed his palm against his head and paced. "How is she going to help us if she's here in the United States?"

"She can. And she will. Ms. Stratton is the one to get the ball rolling. For right now, I need all of your contact information, but you will need to leave a message for Ms. Stratton also. It's unlikely she'll answer."

"How long will it be before she calls?"

"I don't know. It could be a few hours, but I assure you, she will call you back. I also need you to give me all of Mallory's contact information, whatever you have."

Tate gave her the address, Mallory's e-mail address, and her phone number. "I think her phone only runs on Wi-Fi, but she said she can't get the Internet to stay connected very long at all. And I think she's piggybacking off . . ." Tate stopped, knowing it was illegal.

"That's fine," the woman said.

"And what did you say your name is?"

"Lisa Peterson." She paused. "Do you have Mallory's passport number? And do you know if she's registered with the consulate in Peshawar?"

"I don't know." Tate shook his head.

"I'm going to pass all of this along to Cynthia also. But you must call her, too, and leave as detailed a message as you can. I know it's hard, but stay by your phone, and she will call you back."

Tate swallowed back a knot in his throat. "Okay. Thank you for your help."

He called Cynthia Stratton, and as Lisa had said, there was no answer. In a shaky voice, Tate left as detailed a message as he could, including all of his contact information and Mallory's. Then he sat back down on the couch and covered his face with his hands again.

"Do you want to pray again?" Verdell put his hand on Tate's back and rubbed it back and forth. It was such a touching, endearing thing to do that Tate wiped a tear from his eye.

"I already prayed," Tate said, wondering if God was hearing him. But he said another quick, silent prayer.

Verdell stood up, and Tate could feel him just staring at him, so he finally looked up. "What, Verdell? What is it?"

He shouldn't have agreed to keep Verdell. He was too on edge to be around a ten-year-old kid. He was ready to snap at anyone.

"Look, I'm just really worried right now, okay?" Tate shook his head, but Verdell just kept staring at him.

"I've never seen you this sad."

Tate gazed back at the boy. "I've never been this sad. The woman I love is in danger. I'm very sad. And worried."

"I—I want to do something to make you feel better."

Tate bit his lip, then took a deep breath. "I know you do, buddy. And I appreciate that. But there's nothing you can do. I just have to wait for that woman's phone call."

Verdell frowned. "I know what it feels like to be really sad."

"I know you do." Tate reached over and touched him on the arm.

Verdell frowned even more, nervously switching his weight from one foot to the other. Then he walked to the piano, sat down at the stool, and put his hands in position. Tate was just getting ready to tell the child that he wasn't in the mood for teaching—and certainly not in the mood to listen to Verdell suck the passion out of a piece of music right now.

But then Verdell began to play Chopin's "Fantaisie"—the Impromptu in C-sharp Minor—and Tate just stared. Verdell played with the passion and enthusiasm of someone who had been playing the difficult piece of music for fifty years. The opus that most seasoned piano players would never master. Verdell played it in a way that Tate couldn't even play it. From memory. Tate didn't even try to stop his tears.

When Verdell was done, he turned to Tate and said, "I think I'm a better piano player than you are."

Despite his sick sense of doom and sadness, Tate smiled.

BETH WISEMAN

"Yes, buddy. I do believe you are." He stood up and walked to Verdell, and Verdell eased his arms around Tate.

"I hope that makes you feel a little better."

Tate dropped to his knees and pulled Verdell close. "It does. Thank you, buddy."

MALLORY STAYED UP MOST OF THE NIGHT TRYING TO get on the Internet again. By three in the morning, she gave up. She was still running a fever, exhausted, and scared. She lay down, closed her eyes, and prayed. When she woke up, the sun was shining brightly through her window. She walked to the door, put her ear against it, and didn't hear anything, so she eased the door open. Still nothing.

She got dressed and made her way onto the landing, then walked slowly down the stairs. It was Saturday, but she didn't hear any movement in any part of the house. She walked to the front door and turned the knob. Locked. She pulled back the blinds and saw that Abdul's car was gone.

"Fozia!" she yelled as loudly as she could. Her fever didn't feel as high, but she was exhausted. When Fozia didn't answer, she went to the third floor and checked all the bedrooms. Empty. Then she went to Abdul's room on the second floor. She'd only been in his room once before, when he was showing her the house. The rest of the time he kept the door closed. Locked, for all she knew. But when she turned the knob, it opened.

He had a king-sized bed, a nightstand, and a dresser. His

room was larger than the other bedrooms. She opened the closet, surprised to see that it was actually smaller than the one in her room. As she walked around the room, she tried to focus on what she was going to do.

No money. No credit cards. And most of the time, no Internet. Even the card from the man at the airport—Frank—was gone. She could break a window and hit the streets, but she recalled her trip to the bank. Even with Fozia at her side, Mallory had been terrified. And she didn't have a key to the gate at the entrance of the small subdivision.

She noticed Abdul's briefcase on the dresser. It was probably locked, but her no-snooping rule no longer applied. She laid her hand on it for a few moments, then clicked the button to open it. As she thumbed through the papers, she realized she couldn't read anything. It was all in Arabic. Just as she was closing it, she saw something in English. Majida's medical records. It only took a couple of seconds to notice the piece of paper taped over the spot for "name." He'd merely taken someone else's leukemia diagnosis and put Majida's name on it.

I have been so stupid. She put everything back like it was and went back to her room.

Where did they go? How long would they be gone? Maybe they were all out running up her credit cards. Ironically, she'd called every credit card company before she'd left and told them that she would be traveling to Pakistan so they could put it on her records and honor any charges.

Or maybe they'd gone and withdrawn the ten thousand

dollars from the bank account, although she doubted it would be available yet. She sat down on the bed and fought the urge to cry. *Think, think.*

Everything but a few toiletries was still packed. She walked back downstairs and looked out the window again. She could see the mangy dog on the other side of the gate. "I wish I could help you, fellow."

She went back upstairs, logged onto the Internet with surprising ease, and found an e-mail from Tate.

I am working to get you out of there, so if anyone from the consulate or somewhere official e-mails you, it's legit. It might be someone named Cynthia Stratton or Sharon Brune, or maybe Lisa Peterson. I PROMISE I will get you out of there. I love you with all my heart. Be tough, baby. Pray. xoxo Tate

She was just about to allow herself a full breakdown when she saw an e-mail from Sharon Brune. She opened it.

Dear Miss Hammond,

Our office received a phone call from a man named Tate Webber who has expressed concerns about your safety. Is this correct?

If you do require assistance from the US Consulate, please let us know. There are specific services the consulate can offer for a US citizen should you require help. Please feel free to reply directly to me at this e-mail address or call the number below.

Also, if you would like for us to remain in contact with your friend Tate, to keep him informed about your situation, please let us know.

Regards,

Sharon Brune

Public Diplomacy/Consular Officer, US Consulate, Peshawar

"Thank you, God! And my Tater Tot!" She hurried to respond.

Yes, please help me. I'm being held here against my will. They've taken my credit cards and money. What should I do? - Mallory Hammond

She hit Send and breathed a sigh of relief when it went through. Less than a minute later, her e-mail chimed.

Hello Mallory,

We are working on it. Do you have a phone number where I can contact you? And can you verify that this is the address where you are at?

The address was correct, so Mallory wrote her back.

I have a phone but no service. Internet goes in and out. The address is correct. Please tell Tate I'm okay. And please, can you send someone to come get me?

She waited, holding her breath that the Internet would stay connected. Another e-mail.

> Mallory,
>
> Is there a way anyone you know could come and take you to the consulate? We are about fifteen minutes by car from the address you are at. Once at the consulate, we have officers who can discuss options with you. The consulate unfortunately does not have resources to extract you from your residence. We are obviously concerned for your safety and well-being, and the best thing would be to get you here to discuss those options.
>
> Sharon

Mallory heard movement downstairs and the heavy door opening, then the sounds of Waleed and Zyiad giggling. She typed as fast as she could.

> I don't have any friends here. The family has been gone, but I hear them returning. I don't trust any of them to help me. Please send someone to get me. I'm scared! - Mallory

She closed her computer, unsure whether to go downstairs or stay where she was. Then she recalled what Abdul had said about her being well for their honeymoon. She quickly crawled underneath the covers and pretended she was asleep, but she heard footsteps approaching. And without even opening her eyes, she recognized Abdul's cologne.

Please, God. No.

CHAPTER TWENTY

Tate woke up on the couch when his phone rang. It was three o'clock in the morning, and once he got his bearings, he saw Verdell asleep on the floor with the television on but muted.

"Hello?"

"Is this Tate Webber?"

"Yes."

"This is Tom Kramer with the US embassy in Islamabad."

Tate walked toward his bedroom. "Do you have Mallory? Is she okay?" He closed the door behind him.

"We're working on it."

Tate turned on his light and blinked his eyes a few times to adjust. "What does that mean?"

"We are working with a woman in Peshawar to get Mallory relocated."

"Sharon Brune? She called me a couple of hours ago, and I verified all of the information I gave to the woman from the Department of State."

"Yes, Sharon has been in contact with Mallory."

"Thank God." Tate sighed. "Where is she now?"

"Well, they don't have her out of the house yet. The problem is, the consulate cannot extract someone from a residence. We need Mallory to get to the consulate. Once she's there, we can give her full protection and help her get back to the United States. She said she doesn't have any friends there?"

"No, she doesn't. Should she take a cab?" Tate was pacing his bedroom.

"No, we don't recommend that. Mallory isn't in a very safe area. Did she realize where she was going to be staying?"

"No. But being in the house with that man isn't safe either. That guy conned her from the beginning, tricked her into marrying him. He told her his daughter had cancer, and Mallory thought that by marrying him she could bring him and his daughter back here for his daughter to get medical treatment."

"Hmm . . . they devise all kinds of ways to lure women over here, but I haven't heard that one before."

"She said in an e-mail that he took all of her credit cards and cash. Can't you arrest him for that?"

"No. We're here strictly to help US citizens who come to us for help. The Pakistani government will not let us intercede in domestic situations. But I wanted to let you know that we are trying to see what we can do to help Mallory. Can you confirm your e-mail address?"

Tom read the e-mail address, and Tate confirmed it. He wondered if Tom was his real name, if people in his and Sharon's types of jobs even used their real names. The guy sounded about Tate's age and didn't have a foreign accent.

"So what now?" Tate asked.

"Just stay by your phone. Sharon is trying to get hold of her. They were e-mailing back and forth, but the last e-mail said that the family was returning home. Then the connection went dead. Try not to worry."

"But I am worried. Please tell me you can get her out and somewhere safe."

"We've checked out the man she's staying with. He isn't flagged in any of our databases. No record or anything."

"So he's not a terrorist or anything?"

"No. He's just a cruel, dishonest man, from the sound of it."

Tate rubbed his forehead. "I applied for a visa in case I need to go find her. But they said it can take anywhere from a week to a month."

"Yeah. It depends. Where'd you apply at?"

"The office in Houston, Texas."

"Okay, but you don't need to hop on a plane just yet. We're working to get her to us, and it wouldn't be safe for you to go to where she's staying."

"I love Mallory. I'll go wherever I need to."

"For now, sit tight and know that Sharon is working on it."

"You keep saying that—working on it. If you can't go physically get her, then . . ." Tate raised his shoulders and dropped them slowly as he shook his head.

"Let me try to find out exactly what is going on. Better to e-mail you or call?"

"Either one. I'll keep my phone with me, and I get my e-mail on it."

"Okay."

They ended the call, and Tate sat down on the bed, wide awake. "Stay safe, Mallory. I love you."

MALLORY NEVER LEFT HER ROOM ON SUNDAY, TERRIFIED that Abdul would want to consummate their marriage, and just the thought made her feel sicker than she already was. She was mostly weak. Twice Fozia had knocked on the door. The first time was to tell Mallory that Abdul said Fozia couldn't take Mallory anything to eat or drink. "If she wants anything, she can come downstairs and be a part of this family," he'd said.

The second time Fozia didn't knock. She walked in, set a full glass of water on the nightstand, and said, "Hide the glass when you're done."

Mallory had refilled the glass several times with water from her bathroom in an effort not to get dehydrated. She waited until everyone was asleep Sunday night and the house was quiet before she got out the computer. As it warmed up, she pressed her palms together and looked up.

Please, dear God, please, please help me to stay connected long enough to get out of here. Please.

There were three e-mails from Sharon.

Mallory,

We are working with an NGO (nongovernmental organization) to bring you to the consulate. However, we will need you to get past the gate that surrounds your cluster of houses, then you will need to walk about five minutes to reach the contact. This is not the most ideal situation, but stay online if you can and wait for us to tell you where to go.

Sharon

She went to the second e-mail.

Mallory,

Please let us know when you are able to leave the house. Your last e-mail said that the family was home. Bring only what you can carry for the five-minute walk. We will wait to hear from you.

Sharon

As she clicked the last e-mail, she wondered how she was ever going to manhandle her heavy suitcase, laptop, and purse the way she was still feeling. But she'd do whatever it took to get out of here. Even if she had to leave everything. The last one read . . .

Mallory,

The NGO has said that the pickup point we first discussed with them is not safe. Please make contact with us

as soon as you can. By the canal at the end of street 6 is a
suitable spot.

Mallory saw that the e-mail was sent hours ago. She
doubted Sharon stayed up all night long, but she sent an
e-mail while she had Internet.

I don't know where the canal at the end of street 6 is. Can
you please tell me how to get there, and I don't know how
I will get past the large gate that surrounds the houses.
Thank you. I'll be waiting to hear, but the Internet is not
good here.

She forced herself to stay up another two hours, but no
e-mails. From anyone. Finally, she lay down to sleep. Hopefully
tomorrow would be a big day and she'd say good-bye to this
place forever. She thought about Majida, how she'd come here
to save a life. And failed. She'd been fooled by Abdul. Lost ten
thousand dollars. And now she was a prisoner in a dangerous
part of the world. At least it sounded like help might be on
the way.

She stayed in bed Monday morning until she heard
Abdul's car start, then she tried the Internet for the next hour.
When it wouldn't connect, she finally got dressed and went
downstairs. Majida was sitting on the couch, and Mallory
could hear Fozia in the kitchen. She didn't say anything to
Majida but walked straight into the kitchen.

"Nice outfit." She leaned against the counter. "Which one
of my credit cards bought it?"

Fozia hung her head, took a deep breath, and looked up at Mallory. "I am wearing it because Abdul asked me to. And I think you should just be grateful at this point that he visited my room during the night and not yours."

Mallory was quiet for a few moments, unsure how much to trust Fozia. "What is Abdul's plan? He can't just keep me locked up here forever. Doesn't he think someone will come to get me? My parents? Tate? Someone?"

"I don't know his plans or intentions." Fozia squeezed water out of a soaked rag and started wiping down the counters. Finally, she looked up at Mallory. "I'm sorry Abdul found out about the money. Now Majida has no way to get away from here."

This sounded to Mallory like a plea for more money. She folded her arms across her white blouse. She had on jeans today, saving her last clean shalwar and kameez to make her escape in. "What's Abdul planning to do with the ten thousand dollars?"

"I have no idea. You should have never told him how much money you have."

"I didn't say how much." She paused. "Does he think I'll just keep transferring money to that account?"

Fozia sighed. "Mallory, I don't know what Abdul will do from one day to the next. Just try to be kind around him. Don't stir up trouble."

"Someone will come for me."

She decided not to say anything else about it. Fozia looked up at her with swollen eyes.

"I hope that someone does come for you. I hope that you

make your way safely back to the United States. You should never have come here."

"Yet you were in on the plan from the beginning."

"Yes." Fozia tossed the rag into the sink. "Only to the point of you marrying Abdul and getting him to the United States. I wouldn't have taken your money."

"You *did* take my money."

"For my daughter!"

They both turned toward the entrance into the kitchen when they heard footsteps.

"Can you both please stop yelling?" Majida hung her head and put her hands across her stomach.

Fozia walked to where she was standing. "Are you feeling worse?" She put a hand on Majida's arm, then turned to Mallory. "She was throwing up this morning, so she stayed home from school."

"No. I feel the same," Majida said.

Mallory walked closer. "How far along are you?"

Fozia answered. "She is five months pregnant."

Mallory's jaw dropped. "That far? And she hasn't seen a doctor?"

Majida and Fozia both looked at Mallory, but Fozia responded. "No. It wouldn't be safe for anyone to know that she is with child. Only my brother knows. I trust him, but he cannot help us."

"Ammi . . ." Majida blinked her eyes a few times as she spoke to her mother. "I think there are two."

Fozia frowned. "Two what?"

Majida glanced at Mallory, then back at Fozia. "Two babies."

"There's no way to know that," Fozia said as she put a hand on Majida's stomach.

"There are two," Majida said again. "I can feel them."

Mallory had a friend who had twins. She'd known she was having two before an ultrasound confirmed it. Just gut instinct, she'd said. "What are you going to do now? About the pregnancy."

Fozia spoke to Majida in Pashto. Mallory was starting to recognize the differences between Pashto and Urdu, even though she didn't understand either. Majida left the room. Fozia turned to Mallory. "I don't know. I cannot send her out into the world with no money and nowhere to go."

"She has a place to go. She can go to Soraya's parents' house."

"So I just send her out on her own with nothing?"

"That seems safer than her staying here and being killed by your crazy husband." Mallory folded her arms across her chest.

Fozia folded her arms across her chest also as they faced off. "He's your crazy husband too."

"Not for long." Mallory turned and headed back upstairs to try to connect to the Internet. When she finally succeeded on the fifth or sixth try, she found an e-mail from Sharon saying to stand by for further instructions.

After two more hours, she was still online. But no e-mails. She'd e-mailed Sharon and Tate, and she was starting to panic when she didn't get any responses. She didn't want to be here one more night under the same roof as Abdul. She glanced at the clock, knowing the kids would be home from school any minute. A couple of hours after that, Abdul would be home. She had less than four hours to get away. Then she remembered the locked gate.

Dear God, please help me.

She prayed for the next hour, still unclear if she was doing it correctly. But when she prayed she felt hopeful, different somehow, and it did make her want to know God better.

She waited to hear from Sharon, but she was terrified she'd lose the connection and not be able to get back on. And then what? As she stared at the screen, her heart pounded. Finally, her e-mail chimed, and there was a message from someone named Tom Kramer.

Hello Mallory,

I am with the US Embassy in Islamabad. I am working with Sharon Brune to get you to a safe location. Sharon is in Peshawar, and she is having Internet problems. Is there a phone number where we can reach you? We are working to see what options are available.

Sincerely,

Tom Kramer

US Embassy, Islamabad

Mallory's hands were shaking as she typed.

No phone. And I don't know how long I will have Internet.

She hit Send just as she heard the front door open and the boys' voices. That meant only two hours until Abdul was

home, and her chance to get out of the house would be gone.
She doubted Fozia would try to stop her, but she would have to
get Fozia to give her a key to the door and gate. She waited. For
the next hour and a half, she stared at the computer screen—
only thirty minutes left before Abdul was home. Her heart was
racing so fast she felt like she might pass out. And it was nothing short of a miracle that the Internet stayed on.

Then finally an e-mail came from Sharon.

Mallory,

Members of our trusted NGO will pick you up by the
canal at the end of street 6 at 3:45. Bring only what you can
carry. Please let me know what you are wearing and any
other description that will be helpful to the driver. The car
picking you up is a white Toyota Corolla. There will be a
female sitting with the male driver. They will take you to a
safe house, and I will be in touch with you there.

Mallory couldn't stop her hands from shaking as she
read the directions to get to the end of street 6 and quickly
responded.

I will be wearing a green-and-white flowered kameez, white
shalwar, and a pink scarf, with black sandals. I have a black
laptop bag and a black purse. I am leaving now. Thank you!

She hated leaving any of her belongings in this house, but
there was no way she could haul that suitcase. She stuffed as
much as she could of her toiletries and clothes into her laptop

bag and purse and headed down the stairs, and even though she still felt like she might have a low fever, she was moving faster than she thought possible. As she crossed through the living room, she could hear the boys laughing in the basement. She didn't see Fozia or Majida.

"Fozia! Majida!" She started running back up the stairs, calling for Fozia repeatedly. When she didn't see them, she ran back down the stairs.

"What are you yelling for?" Fozia came out of the basement with Majida following her. "We were giving the boys tea and biscuits." She saw Mallory's laptop case and purse by the door. "I asked Abdul what I was to do if you tried to leave. He said you wouldn't be stupid enough to do that, that you knew you didn't stand a chance on your own." Fozia stared long and hard at her. "He's right, you know. You'll be killed on the streets on your own. You don't know where to go, what's safe. It's not even safe for you to take a taxi cab." She paused. "And Mallory, your visa has expired, hasn't it?"

Mallory hadn't even thought about that. At any checkpoint, she could be arrested for the visa that expired today.

"Just give me the key to this door and the one to the gate. Now!" She moved toward Fozia.

"You won't make it, Mallory. Just stay and we will figure something out."

Mallory rolled her eyes but then glanced at the clock. "I don't have time for you to figure something out. Give me the key! Someone is coming to get me. Someone official who will keep me safe and get me out of this country!"

Fozia talked to Majida in Pashto, and when Majida started

to cry, Mallory had no idea what was going on. But Fozia returned with two keys and handed them both to Mallory.

"Take Majida with you!"

Majida latched onto her mother's arm. "No, Ammi. No!"

They went back and forth for a minute in Pashto, and Mallory finally said, "I'm going. And I can't wait." She put the key in the lock, picked up her laptop and purse, and hurried out the door.

"Wait! Take her with you."

Mallory didn't turn around. She kept her eyes focused on the gate, and she could see the mangy dog waiting for her on the other side.

Fozia hollered her name again, then said, "You said you wanted to save a life! You still can."

Mallory froze in her steps, then turned around. Majida wouldn't let go of her mother. Mallory left her belongings in the sandy driveway and ran back.

"Majida. You can't think about yourself right now. You have a baby to save. Maybe two. If you really and truly believe that your father will kill you, then come with me. It's your only chance." Mallory knew that Abdul would be driving up any minute. "You must decide now, Majida. I'm leaving."

Mallory took off running, and when she turned around, Majida was following her. Fozia was on her knees weeping. Mallory locked eyes with Fozia, knowing the woman would never see her child again or know her grandchildren.

Mallory swung the gate open as the dog stood to one side and watched, then she and Majida ran to the pickup spot. The white Corolla was already there.

CHAPTER TWENTY-ONE

Mallory handed over her laptop, cell phone, and eight dollars that was in the side pocket of her purse. She'd forgotten it was there until the woman in charge of the British safe house asked her to empty everything out on the table. Abdul had taken the other six hundred and some change in her wallet.

Majida had cried all the way to the safe house, which was about two hours away. Mallory wasn't sure what Majida was more upset about—having to leave her family or the possibility of her father finding her. She wondered what Fozia would tell Abdul about Majida. It would be too coincidental that Majida left when Mallory did. Hopefully Fozia would blame it on Mallory and spare herself another beating.

Dot Smith—at least that's what the woman's name tag read—asked Mallory to fill out some paperwork. Dot looked to be about Mallory's mother's age, except that this woman didn't bother dyeing her gray hair. She wasn't overly friendly, but nice enough that Mallory felt safe. She had a British accent and talked very softly.

"Are you sure that Majida will be okay?" Mallory asked as Dot took back the papers.

"Yes. We have already spoken to the people who will be taking her in, the Durranis. Apparently their daughter called to tell them that a young pregnant girl might be coming to stay with them. And we have a doctor coming to check on her before she travels to Lahore."

"Will I be riding to Lahore with Majida?"

"I don't think so. They will probably try to get you a flight out of Peshawar or Islamabad."

"I don't have any money with me, and all my credit cards were stolen." She briefly wondered how much had been charged on the cards.

"The embassy will work with you on all that."

Mallory sat quietly for a minute while Dot finished writing. "Is someone going to be able to let my boyfriend and family know that I'm okay? And do you know how long I'll be here?"

Dot stood up, walked to a file cabinet, and pulled out a blank file. She wrote Mallory's name on it, then stuffed the paperwork inside. "I'll talk to Sharon and ask her to let your relatives know that you are safe."

Am I? Will I ever be?

It was a small office with one desk, the chair Dot was using behind the desk, and two worn chairs across from her. It was musty, damp, and cold.

"I'm going to show you to your room. You'll be by yourself

without a roommate. We group according to age, and there isn't anyone here your age. Plus, you said you think you've had a fever within the past twenty-four hours."

Mallory was glad she didn't have to make small talk with a stranger, but she knew Majida was afraid and wished she could have roomed with her. She also wished she had her computer or phone. "Not allowed," Dot had said. "For the safety of everyone here, we hold all modes of communication. We don't want anyone divulging our location."

Mallory had briefly tried to argue, insisting she didn't even know where she was, but it was a rule Dot was not going to bend on. No men allowed at all. Even the man who picked her up. They'd switched drivers halfway into the drive, and the woman passenger in the Corolla—who'd called herself Anne—dropped the man off somewhere along the way once she said they were past all the security checks. He'd called himself Bob. Bob wasn't even allowed to know where the safe house was, and he was a trusted member of the NGO.

"Sharon Brune will be in touch with us to let us know when she can get you a flight out of the country and back home again." Dot motioned toward the door. "I will show you to your room now."

"Can you let me know how Majida is doing also?"

Dot nodded, then used a key to unlock the door, and Mallory walked inside.

TATE LISTENED TO WHAT TOM KRAMER HAD TO SAY, then he hung up his phone so he could relay the message to the group. Mallory's parents, Vicky, her kids, Tate's mother, and Verdell were all gathered in Mallory's parents' living room. They'd gotten word that a car was being sent for Mallory, and they'd been together for several hours, waiting for word that Mallory was safely out of "that maniac's house," as Mallory's father had been calling it.

"She's at a safe house, and she's okay. That's all the guy at the embassy in Islamabad could tell me. They don't let any men know the location. They're working on scheduling a flight, but it might be a few days before she can leave. And for the safety of all the women there, she can't have any means of communication, her phone or laptop." Tate picked his phone up. "I need to send Soraya a text to let her know Mallory is okay."

Mallory's father grunted, but Tate ignored him. He'd been making snide comments all afternoon, and while Tate mostly agreed with everything Melvin Hammond said, Tate didn't think the language he used was appropriate for any of the kids to hear. And he didn't agree with the man's thoughts about all Muslims. Soraya was as nice a person as he'd ever met, and her own life had been shattered because of all this. She texted him back right away: I'M SO GLAD SHE'S SAFE. PLEASE KEEP ME UPDATED.

FOR THE NEXT TWO DAYS, TOM KRAMER STAYED IN touch with Tate, assuring him that Mallory was fine, but Tate wished he could hear that from Mallory. He'd been forwarding all the messages he received to Mallory's family, his mother, and Soraya. But Tate couldn't seem to get his nerves settled. He'd barely eaten, and he'd been snapping at Verdell.

Verdell. The miraculous piano player. When he'd told Chantal about Verdell finally playing, she just said, "See, I told you he could play." Chantal was still in Oklahoma and wasn't offering up any information about when she would be back, but at least she was calling to check on her nephew.

The kid couldn't just "play." That was the largest under-statement Tate had ever heard. Verdell played better than Tate already. He would be a monster piano player by the time he was an adult.

Tate looked at his watch, struggling to stay up until almost midnight, which was when he usually heard from Tom. Verdell had been asleep for a couple of hours when Tate's e-mail chimed.

Hi Tate,

We have booked Mallory on a flight for Thursday. She will leave from Bacha Khan International in Peshawar, then travel to Dubai, through Chicago, then to Houston. Arrival at Bush Intercontinental will be Saturday at two o'clock in the morning. I will get you all the flight numbers, and I will pass along details as I receive them, but I am assured Mallory is doing well.

Best regards,

Tom Kramer

Tate wrote back.

Thanks, Tom. We are all anxiously awaiting her safe arrival, and we appreciate you keeping us informed. Do you need a credit card for the flight?

Tate had already checked his credit card balance, and he was pretty sure he had enough to pay for the flight. Tom's e-mails usually came quickly at this time of night—which was Tom's daytime.

Tate, we have secured the ticket. Mallory will sign a government note for the cost, and when she arrives in Chicago she will have to hand over her passport to authorities. It will be returned to her when she pays off the note. This is the easiest way for us to do things at this point.

Tate finally dragged himself to bed. And said lots of prayers.

Ismail listened to Abdul screaming from the other side of the world, and when his cousin was done, Ismail said, "I am sure Mallory didn't *steal* your daughter."

Soraya refused to see Ismail, but she'd texted him that Mallory was in a safe house. No one said Majida was with her, but everyone speculated that she was. Even Abdul.

"She is no good woman, Mallory. I make her my wife, to promise taking care of her, and she runs away and takes my Majida."

"Why are you even telling me this? I want nothing to do

with you, Abdul. I'm sorry Majida is missing, and I hope that she is okay, but you have ruined my life." Ismail paced across his living room. "Lies and betrayal. You have no honor."

"Where is Majida?" Abdul yelled loudly into the phone.

"I have no idea. And I'm hanging up."

Ismail hit End and tossed the phone onto the couch. There had to be some way for him to make things right, to get Soraya back. But he wasn't sure he'd ever be able to face Mallory.

He paced some more, then prayed for Mallory and Majida. If Abdul found out the girl was pregnant—and had brought shame upon his family—he would go to the ends of the earth to find her. And kill her. This much he knew about his cousin.

MAJIDA HAD SPENT THE LAST TWO NIGHTS IN THE other bed in Mallory's room. Dot had finally allowed it because Majida was so upset and they were concerned. They hadn't talked much, mostly because they were both exhausted. But what little Majida did say was about her father, and how fearful she'd always been of him. But the light amid it all was that the doctor had confirmed that Majida was having twins.

It was going to take a long time before Mallory would forgive herself for being duped by a man like Abdul. But mostly she just wanted to fall into Tate's arms. Sharon Brune had been to the shelter twice. Once to make sure she was okay, and the second time to let her know the flight information.

Mallory packed the few things she had, then she sat down on her bed, knowing it would be hard to say good-bye to Majida.

"Will I ever see my mother again?" Majida was sitting on her bed facing Mallory as she blinked back tears.

"I don't know." Mallory tried to imagine what that would be like. "Maybe somewhere down the line you'll feel safe and be able to contact her." She paused. "They are coming to get me in a few minutes. You know I would take you with me if I could."

Majida nodded. Through her tears, she said, "I will miss my mother and brothers." Mallory nodded, but Majida wasn't done. "Mallory, you wanted to save a life. Well, you saved my life and the life of my babies. You saved three lives."

Mallory thought about how the Internet had stayed on for so long so she could escape, and about the way things had ultimately worked out for Majida. For the first time in her life, she gave credit where credit was due. To God. She couldn't have foreseen His plan.

"I will be praying for you, Majida. And hopefully someday in the future, I will be able to see your beautiful babies."

Majida started to cry. "Will my babies ever see Anwar, their father?"

Mallory answered honestly. "I don't know." She walked to where Majida was sitting on the bed, then latched onto her hand. "Be strong. Be brave. And pray. My friend Soraya is a wonderful person, so I have no doubt that her parents are going to take very good care of you and keep you safe. I've heard they have a beautiful home too."

Mallory hugged Majida, and the girl held on to Mallory like she might never let go. Mallory kissed her on the cheek, then slowly eased herself away and stood up. Then she said another quick prayer for Majida as she waved good-bye and headed to Dot's office.

She put her phone and eight dollars in her purse and thanked everyone she'd met at the safe house, especially Dot.

"They're here." Dot pointed out the window of her office.

Mallory swallowed the knot in her throat, then hugged Dot and thanked her one last time. Then she went out to the sleek black car with embassy plates. Sharon was waiting, along with two armed soldiers. Mallory didn't care if she ever saw another armed guard in her life.

"Ready?" Sharon asked.

"Very ready," Mallory said before she crawled into the backseat with Sharon. "And thank you for everything." She swiped at her eyes when she couldn't hold back anymore. "I feel so stupid."

"Honey, this happens more than you would think. Very bright women are fooled by these men. They can be very charming, but they aren't at all who they say they are. Most of them just want to get to the United States for a better way of life." She paused. "And there are those few who are involved in other things. Really bad things."

"But you don't think Abdul is one of those men?"

Sharon shook her head. "No. He isn't in our database. Not even so much as a traffic ticket. But that doesn't mean that he isn't a bad man." Sharon smiled. "But it sounds like you have a great guy back home waiting for you."

Mallory sighed. "I do. Tate. I love him very much. This was a stupid thing to do, to come here. The only thing I ever wanted to do was to help Majida."

"And you did."

They were quiet for a few minutes, then Mallory asked, "Do you think Abdul really would have killed her?"

"I don't know. But she thinks so. And her mother thought so. It happens, honor killings."

"Do they end up going to jail when something like that happens?"

Sharon shrugged. "Sometimes. But usually not. The families are usually the ones who kill their own children, or they have a close family member do it. There is nothing more important to these people than honor."

"And I find that so incredibly ironic." Mallory shook her head.

"Now listen. About your flight. The security checkpoints will be nothing like what you've been through so far. Getting out of here is much tougher than getting in. They'll do all the normal pat-downs, but there are certain stations that check for drugs, another one for bombs. I haven't flown out in a while, so I'm not sure about all the procedures, but it will take you a couple of hours to go through it all."

She handed Mallory a phone and a card. "I got you a to-go phone. It only has about fifteen minutes on it, but since you haven't been able to get your phone to work, I want you to have a way to call me if there is a problem.

"My number is on the card. I will keep my phone right beside me until I know you are in the air. If I haven't heard from you, I'll assume you're on the plane. I want you to please call or e-mail me when you have reached the United States. I'm sorry we are routing you through Chicago to get there, but we're required to get the cheapest flight. And remember, you'll need to turn over your passport when you get to O'Hare. To get it back, just pay off the note."

Mallory felt like she couldn't say thank you enough. "I will call you as soon as I get home."

When they got near the airport, the driver didn't turn into the parking lot, and he bypassed the security checkpoints outside the airport. Instead, he drove up to the front of the airport.

"This is where government and dignitaries are dropped off," Sharon said. "I won't be able to go in with you."

They both stepped out of the car when the doors were opened for them.

"This entrance is actually for government only. You're going to have to walk about a hundred yards that way." Sharon pointed to her left. "We will wait here until you are inside." She reached into her purse. "Here is four hundred rupees, in case you need it for anything."

Mallory hugged her, thanked her again, then started toward the entrance Sharon had pointed out. She could see Sharon watching as she showed the guard at the entrance her passport and embassy paperwork with her ticket information on it. She gave a quick wave as her stomach churned. Much as they'd done upon her arrival, people were staring, but this part of the airport had many more armed guards than when she'd arrived.

A guard who spoke fairly good English told her to go to the first checkpoint, the drug check. She put her laptop and purse on the counter, and two soldiers went through her few belongings, chuckling as they did, though Mallory had no idea what was funny. She just stood quietly. She was wearing a blue-and-teal-colored kameez with blue shalwar, and her head was covered with a blue scarf, but without her sunglasses, there was no mistaking she was American.

"Go there next." The skinny guard who had done most of the laughing grinned at Mallory and pointed to his right. Mallory took her things and did what he said, and she was sure every armed guard in the area was watching her.

She went through the same process at the arms and explosives checkpoint, but this time there was no laughing. Instead, the two male guards spoke to each other in Pashto. It took longer at this counter, and Mallory was weak in the knees. She wanted to call Tate, for him to reassure her that everything was going to be okay, but she wasn't sure if she needed an international code and recalled Sharon saying there were only fifteen minutes on the phone. She really just wanted to get all of this screening over and done.

Finally, she was cleared, and the guard pointed to the screening area, which looked a lot like the security area at the Houston airport. As her bags passed by her on the conveyor belt, Mallory walked through the metal detector, praying she wouldn't set it off. She was stopped on the other side by a male guard who sent her to a large woman standing a few feet to Mallory's left. The woman began to pat her down. By now Mallory was shaking, sure she'd be deemed a threat to society and locked up somewhere in this horrible country. But the guard waved her on and she got her things, unsure where to go next. Mallory turned back to the female guard who, despite the full pat-down, seemed the least threatening.

The male guard still had her passport. He stared at it for a long time, then said, "You will need to go get a copy of your passport made."

Mallory swallowed hard. "Why?" she squeaked out.

"We are taking note of all Westerners traveling in and out of Pakistan."

She looked around, thinking that no one had taken note of her when she arrived. "Where do I go?"

"Over there. It will cost you five hundred rupees."

"I—I only have four hundred rupees left." She willed herself not to cry when the guard just shrugged. "Can I pay with American dollars?"

"Yes."

She went to where the man told her to go, paid to have a copy of her passport made, then returned to the ticket counter. Her flight was leaving in less than an hour, and she was fourth in line. Her heart thumped in her chest as she waited.

The same guard looked at the copy for a long while, glancing up at Mallory, then back at the passport and embassy paperwork. He spoke to another guard in Pashto. She recognized only one word in the conversation—*American*. Her pulse raced.

Please, God, get me home.

The guard instructed her to place her hand on the ink pad in front of her, and after she'd been fingerprinted, he finally sent her to the immigration deportation exit.

Mallory gave them the copy of her passport and paperwork,

showing that she'd cleared each station. A much younger male guard stared at her for a long time. She had the strangest feeling he knew her name somehow, and she began to envision Abdul coming into the airport and dragging her out by her hair, never to see home again. She pushed the thoughts away, and finally the guard stamped her paperwork and smiled. "Safe travels."

It seemed sincere enough. "Thank you," she said as she went in the direction he pointed. She endured another pat-down, and two more guards went through her laptop bag and purse. Then they stamped two small luggage tags, attached them to her two carry-on items, and told her where to wait for boarding.

Two guards were standing at the entrance of the lounge. As she peered around them, she could see people sitting and chatting, sipping coffee. Mallory just wanted to sit down and have a glass of water. She looked at her watch. The entire process had taken two hours. But her plane still wouldn't board for another fifteen or twenty minutes.

A soldier checked her ticket, stamped it, and added another stamp to her laptop bag and purse. Finally, she made it to the lounge area and plopped down in a chair next to the only two women she saw. They spoke English with a British accent, and Mallory hoped they would be on her flight. She thought of Frank, who had given her his card three weeks ago when she'd landed in Peshawar. That seemed like a lifetime ago.

She listened closely when a voice came over the loud-speaker. Time to board. So much for rest and water. She pulled her laptop bag onto her shoulder, latched onto her purse, and stood up. She'd only taken a few steps when the English woman rushed up beside her.

"You dropped this."

Mallory took the stamped luggage tag from the woman, then glanced at her purse. "Thank you so much. It must have fallen off."

The woman smiled and returned to her seat, and Mallory stuffed the tag into her purse. So much for female traveling companions.

Mallory followed three men down a ramp to the exit leading to the concourse, where they would catch the bus to the plane.

Two more soldiers. Another checkpoint. Mallory waited. When it was her turn, one of the guards checked the tag on her laptop, then pointed to her purse. "No luggage tag."

"Oh." She reached into her purse. "It fell off." She dug around the small purse. Gum, lipstick, some change, her cell phone, toothbrush and toothpaste, deodorant, hand lotion, and sinus pills Dot had given her to help with her ears on the flight. But no luggage tag. She tried not to panic as the guard repeatedly asked to see the stamped luggage tag for her purse.

"I know I have it. It fell off, and I put it in my purse." She squatted down right where she was and dumped the purse. A line was forming behind her.

"Luggage tag!" This time he yelled.

"I've got it. I know I do." Her hands were shaking as she ran them along the inside of the empty bag. She didn't look up when the two guards chuckled, and when she stood up she was blinking back tears. "I can't find it."

The guard snarled and began talking in Pashto.

"I don't understand." A tear rolled down her cheek, and she quickly wiped it away. "I don't understand," she repeated.

She turned around when someone tapped her on the shoulder. A tall, older man with a very dark complexion, long gray beard, and thick accent asked, "Can I be of some assistance?"

"My luggage tag fell off, and I can't find it. I have to be on this flight." She started to cry, and when the two guards saw that she was sobbing, their expressions softened, and they spoke to the man behind her.

"They said they are sorry, but you will have to go back through the security process."

Mallory grabbed her chest, and the laptop bag slid from her shoulder and onto the tiled floor. "I can't. I'll miss the plane. It took me two hours. I won't make it back in time. Can they hold the plane?"

The stranger put a hand on her shoulder, then spoke to the guards again. After they'd replied, the older man said, "You only have to go back through the x-ray machine." He pointed to a door a few feet to the right of the guards. "They said you can go through there. It is a shortcut."

The man picked up her laptop, handed it to her, and said, "Hurry now."

Mallory glanced at the two guards. They weren't scowling anymore, and they both nodded. She inched her way to the door, put her hand on the knob, and looked back. They nodded again, and before she opened the door, she caught the stranger's eye. "Thank you," she said softly as she left.

It took another fifteen minutes to go through the x-ray machine, but there was not a pat-down, and they tied another tag to her purse. The soldier stamped it, and on shaky legs Mallory hurried back. The guard checked the tag and motioned for her to go to the gates, but she could already see that the buses were gone. There were two men standing near the bus pickup.

"Where are the buses? Are they coming back?"

Both men chuckled. "Yes, they are coming back," one of them said.

She walked away from them, stood by herself, and waited.

But the buses never came back.

CHAPTER TWENTY-TWO

Mallory cried all the way back to the safe house, despite Sharon's words of comfort. But most alarming was the fact that Sharon said they couldn't get her on another flight out for another week. Sharon had been talking to someone at the consulate during the two-hour drive.

"I'm so sorry, Sharon." Mallory had found the missing luggage tag in the side pocket of her purse. The lining was torn, and it had slipped beneath it.

"Honey, I'm sorry for you. I know how much you want to get home."

She looked at her with wide eyes. "Is there another airport? I'll go anywhere I need to. Please."

Sharon sighed. "There is a flight leaving Islamabad in a week. I think it might be a little easier at that airport, but that is the only flight we could get. So you'll have to stay at the safe house until then. But when I take you to the airport in

Islamabad, I'll stay outside until you have cleared all the security check posts."

Mallory nodded, even though she felt like she was going to throw up. She'd waited for over an hour for Sharon to pick her up, and she'd left a hysterical message for Tate, saying she was never getting out of this country. She'd tried to call him several times from the to-go phone, but the call wouldn't go through, and Sharon had lost service too.

"I will personally call Tate and tell him what happened," Sharon said as they finally arrived back at the house. "I will keep him updated on everything. And Mallory, we will get you out of here."

"I just can't stay here another week."

"Honey, you rest. And eat. I am going to take care of everything. I will make sure your family knows what is going on at all times."

Dot met Mallory at the door, and Mallory fell into her open arms. She'd never missed her own mother more than at this moment. She buried her head in the woman's shoulder, and Dot rubbed her back as she stood there and cried.

Once she'd gotten settled back in the same room, she asked about Majida, and Dot told her that she'd left that morning for Lahore. They'd gotten word that she had arrived safely at Soraya's parents' house. It had been the only good news of the day.

Mallory lay down on the bed. Once again she was cut off from the entire world, and she had serious doubts that she was ever going to get out of here alive. Abdul was bound to be livid that both she and Majida were gone.

ISMAIL STARED AT HIS BEAUTIFUL SORAYA FROM ACROSS the table at the restaurant, praising Allah that she had agreed to meet with him. She wouldn't confirm where Majida was. Not that he blamed her. But Ismail had heard her on the phone with Mallory, so hopefully Majida was safe and sound in Lahore.

"What can I do to make this right?" he asked. "I'll do whatever you tell me to have your love again."

Soraya stared back at him for a long time. "I love you, Ismail. Real love does not go away overnight. But it doesn't change what has happened."

"I've already transferred a large sum of money, and I'm planning to give it to Mallory when she gets back."

Soraya cut her eyes at him. "She doesn't need your money, Ismail. Mallory and her family have plenty of money." She raised her chin a little. "I am leaving to go to my parents' house."

Ismail sat taller. "In Lahore? No, Soraya."

"Yes. I am going there for a while."

Ismail thought for a few moments. He knew Soraya's parents lived in a fortress with their own armed guards out front. As much as he didn't want her going so far away from him, he knew her father would keep her safe. Just in case Abdul tried to start any trouble. Or Ismail's father. "Okay," he said softly.

"And maybe someday I will trust you again, Ismail." She started to cry. "There is probably something you should know. Tate is in contact with the people from the consulate and embassy. Abdul is now in the system. The people at the embassy said he is flagged. He will never gain entrance into the United States. So I hope all of this was worth it to him. Neither he nor any of his family will ever be granted a visa for travel here."

Relief washed over Ismail. "When do you leave?"

"I wanted to wait until Mallory got back, but after speaking with my mother, I have decided to leave in three days."

"What about your business?"

"Vanessa and her husband are quite capable of running it for now." She paused, narrowing her eyebrows. "And I trust them to do so."

Trust and honor were huge to Soraya, and Ismail had disappointed her on both counts.

"I will help my mother with some issues she has going on at the moment, and it will take both of our efforts to notify everyone that the weddings are off."

"I will fix this, Soraya. I will have you back in my arms, loving me, respecting me."

"I hope so." She reached for her purse on the floor. "I have to go."

"We haven't even ordered." Ismail picked up the menu in front of him, but then he stood when Soraya did.

"I'm not hungry." She walked around to Ismail, kissed him on the cheek, and blinked back tears. "I will be in touch."

"I won't see you before you leave?"

She looked into his eyes and shook her head sadly. "No."

Ismail watched the love of his life walk away, and he resolved to do whatever it took to get her back. Anything.

WHEN SHARON SHOWED UP A WEEK LATER, MALLORY
felt like a beaten-down woman with little hope of ever getting
back to the people she loved. Her vision had gotten blurry a
couple of days after she'd arrived, so Dot had called in a
woman on her list of trusted physicians to check out Mallory's
eyes. The doctor suspected that Mallory was vitamin B defi-
cient because of her diet, or recent lack thereof. Mallory was
just glad to know she hadn't been poisoned.

As they neared Islamabad, she was terrified about going
through another grueling round of security checks alone, terrified she'd miss yet another flight. Sharon assured her that
things would be much different this time. They'd be stopping
at the embassy first, on the way to the airport, which only
made Mallory more anxious about not getting through all the
checkpoints in time.

She glanced down at the outfit she was wearing, knowing
she was going to burn all of these clothes along with any other
memories she had of this experience. Sharon walked with her
toward the entrance, which of course was guarded by soldiers.
She recalled the evacuations of a lot of US embassies only
a couple of years ago over Al Qaeda threats. Islamabad was
one of them. She wasn't going to feel safe anywhere until she
landed on American soil.

Mallory had tried to call Tate repeatedly from Sharon's
phone during the hour-long trip from the safe house to
Islamabad. Never an answer. Straight to voice mail. Maybe
he'd given up on her. Maybe they all had. Despite all the

sleep she'd had in the safe house, she felt like she could sleep forever.

Sharon pulled the big glass door open and motioned for Mallory to go ahead of her. A young man about Mallory's age walked toward her, smiling.

"This must be Mallory." He extended his hand. "I'm Tom Kramer. I've been looking forward to meeting you." He motioned to a desk with two chairs in front of it. "I need you to sign a few things, then someone will take you to the airport. Another American will be traveling with you, so hopefully you won't have near the problems that you did in Peshawar."

Mallory signed everything Tom put in front of her, then slid the papers back across the desk, unable to even come up with polite chitchat. She hoped her traveling companion would be a woman.

"I know you want to get home, Mallory."

She lowered her head and nodded, afraid she might burst into tears. Tom smiled and pointed behind her. "Here is the man who will assure your safe arrival back to the United States."

Mallory turned around—and burst into tears. She stood, barely able to stay on her feet, and ran into Tate's arms. She buried her face in his chest as he held her tightly.

"I promised I'd get you out of here," he whispered, and he started to cry also.

"But . . ." She forced herself out of his arms and gazed into his eyes. "You can only get here by plane."

He smiled. "Yeah. Twenty-six hours total flight time."

"How? How?"

"I bought a ticket. And here I am."

Mallory threw her arms around him and cried even more. "Take me home."

Tom and Sharon had joined them, grinning from ear to ear.

"I wanted so badly to tell you that Tate was waiting for you, but he begged me not to. He wanted to surprise you. He got here three days ago."

"They put me up in a hotel nearby, baby. But I'm packed. My luggage is already in the car. Let's go home."

Mallory said her good-byes to Sharon and Tom, hugging them both, then they went to the car.

"This is Henry," Sharon said as she introduced both Tate and Mallory to the Pakistani driver. Sharon must have noticed the worried expression on Mallory's face. "He has much more pull with the officials at the Islamabad airport than I do, just in case there is a problem." She smiled as she glanced at Henry, then back at Mallory. "He outranks me. You're going to be just fine. Henry will call me if there are any problems."

More hugs and they were finally on their way. "I can't believe you're here," she said as she curled up against Tate and showered him in kisses, not really caring if Henry had to witness any public affection.

"When I found out you missed the plane, Tom helped me to get my visa expedited, and I was on a plane three days later. By then you were already at the safe house, and I couldn't reach you. So I decided to surprise you."

Mallory eased away and stared into his beautiful eyes. "How awful was the flight for you?"

He smiled. "Pretty awful. And I'll be honest . . . I almost couldn't step onto the plane. Once I was off the ground, I took a sleeping pill and zonked out for the longest part of the trip. I never felt sick. I never had problems with my ears. And all I thought about was you."

They were pulling into the parking lot at the airport when Mallory said, "I think I might have to move. I'm not sure I'll ever feel safe again. Abdul knows where I live. And no matter what, he's going to blame me for Majida leaving. I know everyone says he is flagged in the system and can't get here, but I still will worry."

"How do you feel about Chicago these days? Any chance you'd consider going there with me?"

Mallory looked up at him. "But I thought . . ."

"So did I. But the first guy they hired didn't take the job, and I was their second choice. I didn't accept yet. I wanted to see how you felt." He sighed. "And there is a new twist in the plan. It's about Verdell."

Tate told her about the boy's amazing talent and, more importantly, his latest conversation with Chantal. "She wants me to get legal custody of Verdell, whether or not I take the job."

Mallory wrapped her arms around him again. "I want to spend the rest of my life loving you. Forever. I will go anywhere in the world with you and Verdell."

The driver cleared his throat. "Then let's get you both on that plane."

Mallory and Tate both thanked Henry, and he watched as they went into the airport, promising to stay around until he knew they'd made it onto the plane. He instructed someone to put their luggage onto a cart, calling the man by name. Then he handed him an envelope, and somehow Mallory knew that this man would see them through all the security checks and get them on a plane for home.

She latched onto Tate's hand.

Thirty-eight hours, a long layover in Dubai, and they finally landed on US soil—or at least US concrete.

"Thank you for taking care of me and getting me home," she said as the plane taxied on the runway.

Tate smiled. "I promised you I would."

READING GROUP GUIDE

1. Mallory's number one goal is to save a life. Do you have a bucket list? If so, what is at the top, and what motivates you to reach your goal?

2. Tate wonders whether or not he would be a good father. What are some examples that give us insight as to what kind of man Tate is, and thus the type of father he would be?

3. Verdell is grieving the loss of his parents, but he finds comfort with Tate, choosing to live with him above everyone else. Why do you think that is? What did Verdell see in Tate that Tate didn't see in himself, traits that ultimately mold the relationship between the two of them?

4. Mallory is vulnerable when Abdul first reaches out to her, and he reels her in with his charm—and lies. What are some of Mallory's vulnerabilities that Abdul hones in on?

5. How far would you go to save a life? Would you take the

type of risks that Mallory took to pursue your own #1
goal, even if it isn't to save a life?

6. God always has a plan. What are some of the things that
happen in the book that ultimately set up His plan? An
example would be—if Mallory had been able to have a
child, she would not have been considered for a kidney
transplant. Kelsey might have still died, but would Mallory
have fared well? Would she still have a goal to save a life? If
she didn't, what would have happened to Majida and her
twins? Mallory ultimately saved three lives.

7. Did you agree with Mallory's decision to learn about
another religion outside of Christianity? Are we expected
to accept what we are taught by our parents, or is it right
to educate ourselves in an effort to find what fits us best,
whether that relates to Christian-based religions such as
Catholic, Baptist, Methodist, Lutheran, etc. or others outside of Christianity?

8. Things start to go badly for Mallory early into her trip to
Pakistan. What are some indicators that things aren't as
they seem?

9. Fozia makes the ultimate sacrifice as a parent—to save
Majida by sending her with Mallory, knowing she will
probably never see her again, or ever meet her grandchildren. What do you think happens to Majida?

10. Soraya calls off her wedding to Ismail. Was she justified
in doing so? How much did you sympathize with Ismail,
if at all? Do you hope that they will reunite and still get
married?

11. Were Mallory's parents wrong to forbid Mallory to give

her cousin a kidney? Again, things would have worked out completely different had Mallory been allowed to give that gift of life. Whose lives would have been affected?

12. Did you blame Fozia for any of Mallory's troubles? Or was Fozia just doing the best she could to keep herself and her family safe? Was there ever a time when you suspected that Fozia might still be married to Abdul?

A Letter from the Author

Dear Friends,

So many times, my life experiences find a home in my books, and that was certainly the case with *The Promise*. In the real-life version of the story, a special person in my life—let's call her "Laurie"—was seduced into making a trip to Pakistan and subsequently held against her will. Like Mallory, Laurie was motivated by love and her own spiritual journey.

Laurie was held captive in Pakistan for much longer than Mallory. It took her awhile to admit that she was in real trouble. After a severe blow to the back of her head and several credible death threats, she e-mailed me the code word we had established before she left—AMARILLO. Her captor was on his way home and she didn't have much time to escape.

These details in the story were actually experienced by Laurie: the type of charm and lies Abdul used to get what he wanted; the culture in general; the way animals were treated; Mallory learning that Fozia was not an ex-wife; the physical abuse of Fozia and the children; being sick and unable to get to a doctor; Mallory's escape to the car with the NGO people waiting to help her; her stay at the British safe house; the experience at the airport when she lost her luggage tag (even though Laurie did make the flight); vitamin B deficiency; and Abdul's being flagged in the system so that he could never get a visa to the United States.

I always hope and pray that I'm somehow making a difference. I try to do that through the stories I write. From the beginning, I wanted this novel to show that there are good and bad people in every religion. And I wanted to educate women that these things do happen. If this book helps one woman to think twice before falling victim to such a scheme, I'll be grateful.

I hoped this book was going to be a spiritual journey that encouraged peacefulness in all religions. I thought this book would bring closure for those who were involved in Laurie's rescue. And I admit, in some ways I wanted to get in the last word where Laurie's "Abdul" was concerned. But all that changed throughout the course of writing this story.

In my effort to write an inspirational, educational, and entertaining story, God pulled at my heart in a way I couldn't foresee. Did the book give some closure for those of us closely involved? Yes, I think so. Will it touch others? I pray it will. Ultimately, writing this book changed my relationship with Laurie. I have always loved Laurie, and I know she's always loved me. But I couldn't understand her actions.

After working with her for almost a year on this book, I have a much better understanding about her motivations to make this journey. There were things that happened when she was in Pakistan that I never would have known had we not collaborated on this project. So much didn't even make it into this story because in many ways truth really is stranger than fiction.

Authors sometimes talk about being under spiritual attack when they are trying to write. I didn't really know what that was like—until this book. Yes, I've felt challenges while writing other stories that I hoped would glorify God, but the difficulties I faced while working on this project far surpassed those. Not only did I have a rough time with illnesses, vertigo, surgeries, and a host of other things—but my entire family had health issues that kept me on edge. I overwrote the book, had to go through additional rounds of revisions, and for the life of me I didn't think I would ever be able to get Mallory on that plane. Even though I was writing fiction, it felt all too real to me.

After Laurie's Abdul charmed his way into her life, she lost everything she owned and was left with a broken heart. Even so, she said, "I took a leap of faith. I believed him and loved him with all my heart. He might have broken my heart, but not my spirit or the will to be me. I refuse to give him that power."

I'm proud of Laurie, of the woman she is. The e-mails and phone calls between Tate and the embassy and consulate are almost verbatim the conversations that I had with both agencies. A kind man at the embassy in Islamabad (who was instrumental in getting Laurie safely home) told me on the phone, "I don't think I've ever seen a gentler soul walk through our doors for help."

So it is with thanks and praise that I give all the glory to God. And it is with admiration and love that I dedicate this book to Laurie. A brave—and gentle—soul indeed.

In His name, sending you all peace and blessings,

Beth

ACKNOWLEDGMENTS

As always, the glory goes to God for setting me on this path, guiding me along this incredible journey, and gifting me with stories to tell.

This book was way out of the box for me, and it was personal since it was inspired by actual events. I'm blessed to have an editor who really pushed me to hit my potential with this story. There were tears, rewrites, more tears, and more rewrites. But without Ami McConnell's brilliant insight, this book would not be what it is today. Her encouragement helped me to grow as a writer, and I appreciate her as my editor and my friend. Thank you, Ami! I was "brave." :)

LB Norton deserves a big thank-you also. As line editor, LB took over where Ami left off and cleaned things up. LB, I love working with you!

To my agent, Natasha Kern . . . wow. I don't even know

where to start. There is much to be thankful for where you are concerned. I could fill up pages, I think. So, let me just say, I love you. I admire you. I appreciate you. And I'm blessed to have you with me on this wonderful journey.

A novel is always a group effort, but it helps to have the most amazing publishing team on the planet. To the folks at HarperCollins Christian Fiction—a huge thank-you. And a special thanks to Daisy Hutton for her hands-on involvement through every phase of this project.

To author and speaker Nonie Darwish, as the real-life story unfolded, you were a godsend for sure. Thank you, my friend, for educating me and hand-holding me when I needed it the most.

To the folks at the U.S. Consulate in Peshawar, U.S. Embassy in Islamabad, and the U.S. Department of State. Your swift and effective work on our behalf, and the kindness you showed us then, will never be forgotten.

I've had tons of support from friends and family as I pushed forward with this project, so a huge thank-you to all of you. Especially my husband, Patrick, who was the one dealing with my crybaby tantrums during my rewrites. You rock, dear, and I love you very much.

Brooke has only loved one man.
Owen's heart is filled with bitterness.
Can a mysterious house bring them together
for a second chance at love?

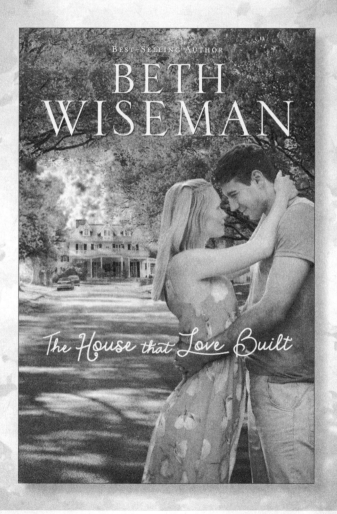

Please join us for A Year of Weddings

ABOUT THE AUTHOR

Photograph by Saxton Creations

Award-winning, bestselling author Beth Wiseman is best known for her Amish novels, but her most recent novels, *Need You Now* and *The House That Love Built*, are contemporaries set in small Texas towns. Both have received glowing reviews. Beth's highly anticipated novel, *The Promise*, is inspired by a true story.